FURRY
FRIENDS
forevermore

FURRY FRIENDS

forevermore

A HEAVENLY REUNION
WITH YOUR PET

GARY KURZ

CITADEL PRESS
Kensington Publishing Corp.
www.kensingtonbooks.com

For all who, like me, have lost a beloved pet, but believe
that God has provided for all of his creatures;
that they are indeed eternal living souls
as the Bible teaches—lift up your head and look to the future
with great anticipation
For they are not gone; rather, they are gone on ahead,
and we shall catch up to them one day.
Of this we can be certain.

CITADEL PRESS BOOKS are published by

Kensington Publishing Corp.
119 West 40th Street
New York, NY 10018

Copyright © 2013 Gary Kurz

All Kensington titles, imprints, and distributed lines are available at special quantity discounts for bulk purchases for sales promotions, premiums, fund-raising, educational, or institutional use. Special book excerpts or customized printings can also be created to fit specific needs. For details, write or phone the office of the Kensington special sales manager: Kensington Publishing Corp., 119 West 40th Street, New York, NY 10018, attn: Special Sales Department; phone: 1-800-221-2647.

CITADEL PRESS and the Citadel logo are Reg. U.S. Pat. & TM Off.

First Citadel printing: May 2013

10 9 8 7 6 5 4 3 2 1

Printed in the United States of America

CIP data is available.

ISBN-13: 978-0-8065-3617-0
ISBN-10: 0-8065-3617-9

Contents

Introduction   vii

1. God Loves His Creatures   1

2. Why Do Animals Suffer?   15

3. Animals Are Eternal Souls   23

4. What Is This Place Called Heaven?   32

5. What Is Heaven Like?   39

6. When Will Heaven Begin?   76

7. Our Reunion with God   104

8. Our Reunion with Friends   143

9. The Rainbow Bridge   170

10. Final Thoughts   178

11. Moving, Humorous, and Thrilling Stories
    (About Animals and People)   185

Introduction

Is it really true that animals have souls? Are they really important to God? Has God made a place for them after this life? Will we be reunited with them? What will that reunion be like?

How vividly I remember pondering these questions when my best friend, Samantha, passed away suddenly many years ago. She was a beautiful West Highland White Terrier, my confidante and shadow. She would listen to my problems intently long after friends and family had lost interest in them. And she could console me with just a tender flick of her tiny little tongue on my hand.

She greeted me at the front door when I returned from work and made me feel like there was no one else in the whole world. She would follow me around so closely one might imagine that we were connected with Velcro. She didn't care if I needed a shower or what kind of mood I was in; she was just happy to be with me.

Her passing was very traumatic for me as such an experience is for most people who lose a cherished family pet. What happened to me at church the next day, something that happens much too often to pet lovers, was totally unexpected and almost too much to handle.

"Why, Brother Gary, what seems to be the matter?" my pastor's wife asked as I made my way to my usual pew on Sunday morning. I didn't respond immediately because I just didn't feel like talking. I probably shouldn't have been out in public so soon after losing Samantha, but I thought support from those of like faith might help ease the pain I was feeling.

Before I could respond, she added, "You are always such a happy person and today you look so glum." I sought desperately for something to say. I felt tears welling up in my eyes and knew I had to squeeze an answer out quickly or risk blubbering incoherently as my emotions took over. I quickly blurted out, "My dog died yesterday."

Sure that she heard the quivering in my voice and saw the tears beginning to flow, I waited for the compassionate words I knew only a pastor's wife could find. To my horror, instead of offering sympathy and compassion, she sarcastically, and if I might add, almost gleefully said, "Oh, and I bet you think your dog went to doggy heaven, don't you?"

It was a rhetorical question to be sure. She was not soliciting a response; she was making a statement. She was telling me that she thought animals did not go to heaven. Apparently it was more important for her to express her personal beliefs than to offer comfort.

I didn't know what to say or do, so I resorted to the tactic most people resort to when they find themselves in an awkward and hurtful situation; I chuckled and walked off. I didn't want to chuckle. I wanted to lash out and admonish her for her callousness, but I didn't. I didn't have it in me. It was not that important at the moment. I couldn't handle a confrontation. I wanted to be left alone and so I chuckled and walked away.

Outwardly I erased any sign of hurt or anger toward her, but inwardly I was mortified. She had taken one of the most traumatic experiences of my life and heaped more grief and pain upon it. Her undeserved cruelty was bad enough, but the sentiment she expressed was even more disturbing. I did not agree with her.

At that time, my disagreement with her idea that animals had no afterlife was based upon nothing more than hope and wishes. I had no idea what the Bible said on this matter, if it said anything at all, despite my many years as a student of the Bible and Bible College. Later, through intense, focused study, I would become an expert on the subject; but then my position was fueled by nothing more than raw emotion and hope. In my work since then, I have received hundreds of letters and e-mails from exasperated church-goers who have suffered similar fates at the hands (or words) of their ministers and other spiritual leaders. Sometimes it was from direct dialogue about a specific pet, but more often it was hurtful comments made from the pulpit that suggested animals were not important and did not have souls. Some ministers have even callously joked from the pulpit about dead animals.

I hope that the information that follows in this and other chapters will help heal any wounds you have suffered. If you feel so inclined, you may want to share this information with your spiritual leaders or others so they may be enlightened and not continue to be the cause of hurt for others in their time of need.

I will not spend a lot of time on this. I do not want to get sidetracked from giving a snapshot of what a reunion with our pets might be like. I want this book to be a source of great hope and anticipation for you.

A reunion is definitely coming; in fact, many reunions. The first and most important will be our reunion with God. Some might contend that *reunion* is not the right word because we have never actually met the Lord before, but for anyone saved by his grace, on the day they accepted him as Lord and Savior they knew they had a meeting with him. So, in fact, our next meeting with him will be a reunion.

There will be other reunions as we meet up with old friends and family and share earthly memories. We will have reunions with people we hardly knew on Earth. We will be surprised to hear how important we were to them or how instrumental our testimony or behavior was in changing their lives.

And then there will be the reunions we have with our beloved pet buddies. What a grand time it will be to share the love we once enjoyed together on Earth and to know for certain that our faith in God's providence for them was certain and sure.

Chapter 1

GOD LOVES HIS CREATURES

This chapter title makes a very bold statement. It claims that animals are loved by God. To some, this statement might seem a little outrageous. They believe that animals are relatively unimportant in this world and certainly not important to God. The only time they hear about animals from the pulpit is when the preacher talks about Noah's Ark or animals being sacrificed. In fact, they may point out that the word *animal* doesn't even appear in the Bible. So how can they be important if God doesn't even mention them?

While it is true the word *animal* does not appear in scripture, animals are mentioned in more than just a few passages; hundreds to be exact. Words and phrases like *beasts, creatures, every living thing,* and *things that have breath* are used in lieu of the word *animal,* but they mean the same thing.

Throughout the Bible are teachings that animals are important to God. Animals are living souls; but they are also eternal souls. They don't live only in the here and now, they live forever. God made them that way. He made all life that way. They are assured of an eternity with their creator when they pass from this world. We will discuss this truth in greater detail in chapter three, but first I would like to continue discussing why animals merit God's attention.

Why are they important to God? Why did He make them eternal souls? Why are they assured a place in Heaven? The short and obvious answer is that God loves them. Love is the ultimate motivator. When we love a person or an animal, we want them with us. We want to spend time with them and be a part of their lives. Indeed, we want them to spend forever with us.

Why then do we imagine that God cannot feel the same way? As we learn in the book of Genesis, God finds much pleasure in the life He has created. With His own hands He brought that life from nothingness. By sheer will He formed living creatures. He loved them one and all. He beheld the entirety of His creation and assessed "that it was very good" (Genesis 1:31).

All His creatures pleased Him. And when I say *all*, I mean all; not some, not many, not even most, but all. That pleasure does not end simply because the earthly shell of one of His creatures expires. God is immutable. You may understand that to mean God never changes, but the meaning is deeper. Not only is it true God does not change, but He cannot change. He is perfect. Perfection cannot be improved. God's perfect love is immutable. It simply cannot change. God cannot stop loving His creatures.

For example, and this may shock you, God loves even the wicked Satan and his horde of fallen angels (demons). He hates Satan's sin. He hates that this once beloved cherub, formerly known as Lucifer, sinned against Him. God hates that Satan led one third of the angels in rebellion against Him. He hates that Satan has wreaked havoc upon His prized creation, mankind. But God still loves him. God is love. He is immutable. Therefore, His love is immutable.

If God can love the undeserving and ungodly, how much more is there a place in His heart for his creatures who remain sinless and innocent? God loves His animals. He has always loved them and He always will, because His love is immutable.

Shame on those who presumptuously claim that God's love has a time limit or condition attached to it. They need to revisit I Corinthians Chapter 13 and earnestly consider the characteristics of agape or Godly love. It is quite unlike our own human or eros love. It is perfect and constant love, not fickle and conditional like our own.

God is no less the animals' creator than He is ours. No one could, or at least no one should, argue this point. Without much effort, we can discern from what He says in scripture that animals are important to Him. Their treatment and care are important. Their well-being is important.

While some carelessly relegate animals to nothing more than a food source, God deems them of great worth and extends His love and providence to them. From their creation, we can see the hand of God present with them. A brief review of some major milestones and events documented in the Bible verifies this.

Creatures we call animals were introduced in the book of Genesis during the act of creation. They were made the day before mankind and placed in the Garden of Eden. When man came on the scene, they immediately became His companions.

They were not a food source and not beasts of burden. They

coexisted with the human in a pristine environment void of fear, disease, and death. There was no predator or prey. Man and beast took sustenance from nature; seeds, fruits, and vegetables.

There were no dangers. There were no injuries or wounds. There was no fear one for the other; all lived in perfect harmony. I have often heard the word *tranquility* used to describe that first habitat of man and animal. It is most appropriate and fitting as God had intended the place to be exactly that, tranquil. Man and animal in close bond with each other.

The human/animal relationship was unlike anything we know today. As I pointed out in *Cold Noses at the Pearly Gates*, I believe there was actual oral communication between man and the animals. That is not just a wide-eyed, shot-in-the-dark guess; there is actually strong evidence that this may have been the case. I will discuss this in more detail in a later chapter.

The Garden was a unique place. God had made it for man, but animals were part of it. From the very beginning, God displayed His love and watchful care for what we term His lesser creatures. He emphasized the importance of animals throughout scripture. They are an important part of His creation; His very hands formed them. They are important companions to mankind; helping us in our toils and struggles. They are important to the economy and ecosystems. And the list goes on.

The next significant mention of animals that we come across in scripture is when God clothed Adam and Eve after their sin made them realize they were naked. In Genesis 3:21 we are told that God clothed them in animal skins. Not long after, Abel made an offering unto the Lord of the firstlings of his flock (Genesis 4:4).

The next time animals came into special focus in scripture was at the time of the great deluge or flood. God had Noah build an ark to preserve his family and the variety of animals He would send to enter it.

We all know the story, so I will skip the details and move to the time after the flood. After nearly ten months afloat, the ark came to rest and God made a covenant with Noah to not flood the earth again. God made it a special point to extend that covenant to the animals, a very significant gesture. This shows us that when charting the course of mankind and this world, animals were a major consideration in God's heart and mind.

Strong evidence of God's providential desires for the treatment of animals, even those to be sacrificed, is found throughout the Old Testament books. Social rules and ethics for the humane treatment of animals were established by the Jewish people. Some of the rules instituted brought condemnation to those who mistreated their animals. People were punished for treating their animals badly.

Other passages in the Old Testament allude to the care God gives to His creatures. We are told that what we humans have labeled *instinct* is not instinct at all, but the providential hand of God. God declares that it is He who clothes the animals, He who tells them when to migrate north or south, and He who provides their sustenance.

Moving ahead to the New Testament, we see other examples of God's tender heart for animals. At the birth of His only begotten son, the Lord Jesus Christ, we see that animals were present in the stable where he was born. I do not think it was by chance that the inn was full and therefore that the stables were full as well. I sincerely believe that God desired to have His innocent son born among the innocent animals with as few people in attendance as possible.

It was necessary that Mary and Joseph were there, of course; but we are told of no one else in attendance besides the animals in that stable. The Magi would not come for nearly two years and the shepherds would come to see the babe only after the angelic host announced that Jesus' birth had already taken place. The nativity scenes are cute, but not very accurate.

There are more examples of the importance of animals in the New Testament. When, as an adult, Jesus fasted for forty days in the wilderness, the time many Christian denominations now recognize as Lent, it was not his parents that he spent that time with. It was not his disciples. We are told that he was ". . . among the wild beasts" (Mark 1:13). He spent the entire time with his animals. It does not say, but I suspect they ministered to and companioned him. When he broke his fast, they undoubtedly brought him sustenance, much like the ravens had for the man of God back in the Old Testament.

In Isaiah chapter eleven, the prophet is moved to give us a glimpse of the coming kingdom in which the "Branch" or Son of God shall set up his earthly theocracy. When read in conjunction with the latter chapters of the Book of the Revelation, we see a change in the animal kingdom, a reversion to their original state, if you will. Animals will no longer have the dread or fear of mankind mentioned in Genesis chapter 9. They will once again be tame and have a heart toward companionship with humans. There will be no predator or prey, as former predators shall eat straw like an ox. They will be at peace with each other. We are told that the wolf shall dwell with the lamb, the leopard with the kid and the lion with the calf. What's more, we are told that a little child shall lead these fierce creatures.

There are other examples that we could site, but I believe these should be sufficient to prove that God loves the animals he created. Therefore, I would like to end this discussion of God's love for animals by offering an observation, actually a conclusion, I have made regarding God's tender and loving care for animals. You might balk at what I say, labeling it whimsical. But it is not at all whimsical. I have arrived at this conclusion after more than fifteen years of observing and evaluating the passing of literally thousands of family pets, my own and those of readers.

I believe that God extends a special mercy and comfort to dying animals that humans do not usually enjoy. While I cannot support my conclusion with a specific passage—there is no verse or group of verses that speak directly to this issue—I draw upon my personal experiences and those of readers. I have discovered, or at least determined, that God intervenes in the passing of animals.

Animals seem to face death with an uncanny acceptance that we do not see in people, even people of faith. I have seen a lot of death in my lifetime. I have sat with believers and unbelievers who suffered from terminal diseases. Undoubtedly, those who are certain of their relationship with God usually face their own passing with a more persevering attitude than those who have no such relationship. But even Christians delay their passing as long as they can, exploring every medical and spiritual possibility to try to extend their lives.

Not so animals. However they arrive at the notion that their time has come, when it comes, they display an acceptance and comfort I have seldom seen in people. There is an almost total absence of fear.

Now, when I say there is an acceptance of their fate, I am speaking of animals that are ill, fatally wounded, or aging. I certainly am not talking about healthy animals that are being chased by a predator or animals being pursued by hunters. We all know that they possess a self-preservation mechanism that kicks in. Animals flee danger. They do whatever they can, often doing extraordinary things, to survive. I do not argue this.

But for animals that are dying through natural, and in some cases, unnatural causes, there is an apparent acceptance of their lot. A good example of this would be elephants. It has been documented that dying elephants not only face their impending passing with calm expectation, but are helped to face it by the rest of the herd.

Surviving herd members perform funeral-like rituals for their dead; and often these rituals begin before the passing of the dying herd member. The passing elephant appears somber at the prospect of dying, but accepting as it is ministered to and guided by the matriarchs of the herd. Once the creature passes in what seems to be the place of choosing, the matriarchs and immediate family members surround the fallen, gently touching the corpse with their trunks and eventually covering it with leaves and branches.

Do not be misled by the mention of a place of choosing for a dying elephant. This only means that when an elephant is awaiting death, a place in the immediate area is selected over others.

The notion that aging or ailing elephants make a pilgrimage to a pre-determined graveyard site where all elephants go is a myth whose origin was probably the earliest Tarzan stories. They do not. But they do recognize and accept impending death with calm and dignity in a type of elephant hospice environment.

Closer to home, I have witnessed my own pets and those of friends, who accept their situation quietly and if I might be so bold to say, fearlessly. Most recently, my Missy, a sixteen-year-old West Highland White terrier, passed in such a way. It tortured me to see her wane and pass, but she handled it all with grace and calm.

Missy was the puppy I wrote about in *Cold Noses at the Pearly Gates* that helped me through the losses of two other wonderful, beloved pets. She was instrumental in my recovery, breathing happiness and purpose back into my life like a healing balm.

It is hard to accept that this wonderful puppy lived her life and grew old so quickly, but there is no denying that she, too, is now gone ahead. I miss her terribly, but I will see her again. She stayed with me as long as she could. Though she suffered considerably from her renal failure and other ailments, she never complained and showed no fear. She wanted to stay with me as long as she could and God gave her the grace to do just that. I saw this providential mercy at work in her life just as I have seen it in the accounts many thousands of readers have shared with me. I thank God for the comfort He extends to his animals to allow them to accept their own passing.

There is no doubt that God loves all His creatures. If you have doubts, you have not honestly evaluated the evidence. It is overwhelming. We have God's own words telling us that He is very happy with the creatures He made. We have His instructions on how to treat our animals—the way that He would treat them. We have His testimony that He provides their sustenance and shelter and directs their migrations. Finally, and perhaps most important, we have the record that He holds their souls or essences in His mighty hand.

I want to end this chapter about God's love for His animals with one final story. This one is very personal and up to this point, it has been very private. I had no intention of ever sharing it publically as I felt it was something that best remained between God and my wife and I. To be honest, I wanted to keep it private because I fear that if I do not articulate it correctly, some will scoff in disbelief and I do not wish to feed anyone's skepticism.

Rather, I want to help build faith in readers and highlight God's providence in our lives with regard to animals. But I am willing to take the risk of being bombarded with e-mail about my having a screw loose or being a heretic if this story will help a few.

I assure you that this story is not embellished upon in any way, and it did happen just as I am about to report it to you. For the record, I am a fundamentalist Christian and a Biblicist. I am not given to wild, sensual, or superstitious experiences. In fact, I too am a skeptic when I hear the type of story I am about to share. Still, I know what happened and I believe my conclusions as to what transpired are well within the realm of probability.

The year 2008 was a very tough year for me. I lost my mother in February and my father in October. That was indeed difficult, but I am a realist and know all of us must pass. I was probably more prepared than they were as they both suffered badly from Alzheimer's.

The year was made a bit more difficult that May when my fourteen-year-old Chihuahua Odie developed a severe renal problem. At first, the condition caused her to have mild seizures, but eventually they came with more frequency and severity.

Despite our efforts and having spared no expense, she continued to deteriorate during the months of radical treatments. Soon, the seizures were coming about every fifteen minutes and each one robbed her of more and more motor skills. In very short order, she was unable to stand well and was getting weaker.

Please do not think we allowed her to suffer. The severe symptoms came on rapidly on a Saturday evening; before that they had been manageable. Lying on the bed beside her, my wife and I knew it was time to let her go. We made the decision and wept together as we hugged our little girl.

Although she could barely move, she rubbed her face in my hands and licked them, letting me know that she understood and that it was okay. She mustered the strength to turn toward my wife, I imagine to signal the same message to her. My wife pulled her closer to her and hugged her tenderly and gently.

A moment later, Odie looked over my wife's shoulder into the upper corner of the room. Her back was to me, so I could not see her face; but I saw her back stiffen and her ears go up.

She suddenly jumped backwards, away from my wife and toward me. This little girl, who moments earlier could barely lift her head, jumped nearly three feet across the bed, twisted in midair, and landed almost perfectly in my arms.

I should explain here that Odie was the cowardly kind of Chihuahua. Looking from the picture window at a dog outside, protected by the sliding glass door, she magically transformed into a German shepherd and acted like she could whip the world. But at all other times she was simply cowardly.

In the car, the windshield wipers sent her looking for a place to hide, panting and shaking. Any nonroutine noise from outside made her run, and usually she ran to find me, wherever I happened to be. Thunder was the worst. It didn't matter what time of day or night it was, she was crawling into my face. With no one else and in no other place in the world did she feel safe but with me when the scary sounds came.

So, it was obvious whatever she saw spooked her and she knew exactly where she had to be to be safe. She landed in my arms and looked quickly over her shoulder at the corner of the ceiling she had focused on moments earlier. She was shaking and panting and more unsettled than I had ever seen her.

My wife was astonished. She asked, "Hon, what happened? Odie's eyes got so big. She looked so terrified." I should point out here that my wife is also something of a coward and while she spoke, she was slowly sliding closer to me, keeping a watchful eye over her shoulder. She said it was to help comfort Odie, but I didn't buy it.

As I held Odie close and let her snuggle, all the while assuring her that it was okay and she didn't need to worry, my wife and I analyzed what had just happened. It was clear that something unnatural or supernatural had just occurred.

We decided Odie must have seen an angel. Okay, I know how that sounds. There are a lot of bizzaro zealots out there who claim to hear voices in telephone poles and see the faces of religious icons in grease spots, etc. This was not like that at all. We are not sensationalists. We were not looking for anything like this to happen; it just happened. As a strict Biblicist and theologian, I was skeptical. I entertained every possible alternate idea; that it was another seizure, her medications, a big moth that neither my wife nor I saw, and a host of other ideas that really did not hold water.

None of our ideas fit as well as the angel idea. It is not that big a stretch of the imagination to arrive at such a conclusion. The Bible tells us that we entertain angels unawares. They are among us. Some do God's bidding. Others are our guardians and helpers. And sometimes we have seen them without knowing it.

But as a theologian, I had a problem reconciling that possibility with what actually happened. If it had been an angel, sent to escort Odie to eternity, why would it reveal itself to her in such a manner? And even allowing for that possibility, why would Odie react with fear to an angel of God?

You cannot imagine the thoughts and possibilities banging around in my mind. Because of her fear, I wondered if what she saw was a fallen angel. If so, why would a demon be interested in scaring a poor little dying dog? And why would God allow a demon inside my home, that of a faithful, devoted Christian?

I had to get hold of myself, much like Peter did when the jail gates opened of their own accord to him (Acts 12:10). My conclusion was that Odie had indeed seen an angel, and her reaction was just what you could expect from her in her earthly body. It was how she reacted to anyone she did not know.

Besides, maybe the angel was not supposed to let her see him.

Do angels make mistakes? I suppose they do. Lucifer and his followers sure did. And maybe this one did, too. He certainly did not help the situation, except to encourage my wife and me to strengthen our belief that God indeed loves His animals and that their deaths are precious to Him.

Again, I am not sure I articulated this as perfectly as I could. I am not big on experiences like this happening in this day and age because unlike early Christians, who experienced miracles regularly, we have the Bible in its entirety and the Word is more powerful than any experience. But it happened just like I said. And it gave me a renewed comfort to know that when I let Odie go the next day, an angel was present to usher her to the next life.

Believe my story or not; it is your prerogative. But believe this. God loves His animals. He always has and He always will.

Chapter 2
WHY DO ANIMALS SUFFER?

Having built such a solid case for God's immutable love, we are presented with something of a dilemma. If He loves these wonderful creatures, and if they are sinless and innocent, how could God allow them to suffer so throughout history at the hands of man? ? Why does He not just swoop in and stop the injustices on the spot?

I believe these questions represent the attitude many have toward God regarding injustices and abuses toward animals, but it is important to note the inferred premise falsely draws one's attention to the question *How could God allow . . .* , when in fact, the focus should be on the key words *. . . at the hands of man.*

As posed, the question attempts to make God the villain, when He is not. This is typical human nature; something goes wrong in life and we look for someone else to blame. We often look heavenward and cry out, "Why God, why?" when, if we would be honest, we can trace the problem back to a deliberate action or decision on our part or the part of others.

Abuse of animals is widespread, perhaps epidemic, in our world. *At the hands of man,* from scientific and product experimentation to dog fights and trophy hunting, terror has been perpetrated upon the creatures we share this earth with. Animals, wild and domestic, have suffered at the hands of mankind for as long as there has been recorded history. The shame and guilt sits wholly upon us and not God. We are not all individually guilty, but as a whole, mankind—not God—is responsible for the poor stewardship we have exercised over the animals He entrusted to us.

Still, the questions have been raised and need to be addressed. Why does God allow it? Why does God allow mankind to exact such evil upon His innocent creatures? Even I find myself asking these potent questions on occasion. Each time I visit a shelter or see a report on the news about animals being abused, it breaks my heart. I find myself asking, "Why God? Why do you allow mankind to repay these noble, loving creatures in such a dastardly way?" You see, I am as prone to blaming God as the next person. It is so easy to pass the buck to God in such situations. We all do it. It is human nature.

But the question *How can God allow . . .* demands an answer and I intend to give one. What I say may seem a bit abstract and taking the long way around getting to the point, but please humor me. I think I can provide enough insight to allow us to understand God's reluctance to intervene.

It is difficult to isolate the societal ill of animal abuse without considering the other evils of society (child abuse, rape, murder, theft, adultery, injustice, etc.). Clearly, God does not always intervene in these matters, either. So the scope of the question must be expanded to include all the woes and injustices of society. Why does God allow such evil to befall humanity and yet not intervene?

The quick and easy answer is that while He might not intervene now, He definitely will one day in the future. That is not some pie in the sky pipe dream. The Lord promises that one day He will balance the books. Every sin, every infraction, even every idle word, will be called into judgment by Him one day. We are told in Proverbs 15:3 "The eyes of the Lord are in every place, beholding the evil and the good."

Wow, that is sobering. God is keeping track of even the idle words men and women speak in secret. As we live our lives, it may seem that He is unconcerned or unaware, but He is watching and forgets nothing. And one day, He will call it all into judgment. All the wrongs will be made right and all the injustices healed. That is the quick and easy answer.

The more detailed and complicated answer is that while God undoubtedly would like to intervene, He restrains himself from doing so for a reason. He despises what this world has become. He despises the things we do to each other. If God had His way, we would still be living in the perfect, sinless, trouble-free environment of the Garden of Eden. He wants nothing but peace, tranquility, and blessings for us. He loves us.

But the truth is, it was not God who caused the change of environment that gives us the woeful world we have today. It was mankind. Oh, I am not pointing a finger at Adam or Eve. It is human nature to be selfish and self-centered, to want to do things our way for our own benefit. The warning from God was understood and believed by Adam. He simply wanted to do things his own way, a selfish trait He passed on. We all possess it today.

And so the world continues to be the woeful place mankind chooses it to be. People remain self-centered and selfish. They do things to benefit themselves and those they love, even to the detriment of others they do not know. Some people are worse than others. Some are better. But what we are individually impacts us collectively and we have no one to blame for life's circumstances but ourselves.

Despite all that, we still think God should intervene and not allow evil and injustices. But is that what we really want? Do we really want God to intervene? Do we want Him to make all the decisions in our lives and the lives of others? I don't think so. If we did, we would conform wholly to the teachings of the Bible on topics such as life, work, relationships, raising a family, tithing, worship, etc. But we do not. We prefer to make our own decisions and live our lives the way we want to live.

Who among us does not appreciate having free choice? We ask, "Why doesn't God intervene?" in certain, select matters, but would quickly flip flop and rebel if He were to intercede in other areas of our lives. We want to live our lives the way we choose to live them. We don't want God meddling with them.

It might surprise you to know that God doesn't want that either. God does not want to control us like mindless drones or robots. He granted us free choice. He instilled in us the desire to be free thinking. He wants people to place their faith in Him and to live their lives according to the way He would want them to, but He wants that to be by choice. He loves us and wants to be a part of our lives, but wants that by invitation, not by forced intervention. When you love someone, it has much more meaning for them to want you in their lives, rather than feeling obligated or compelled to do so.

God has two distinct wills—providential and permissive. His

providential will is absolute. It is His forced will. For example, in Exodus, He says, "Thou shall not steal," and that is set in stone. He will not allow variation or change. It is wrong to steal today and it will be wrong to steal tomorrow.

God's permissive will is very different. It is His "allow" will if you prefer. He allows us to make our own choices. We can choose to steal. We are free to make that grave error. God could intervene, but He has already set the standard to be followed and desires that we willingly keep that standard and not steal.

Still, it is our choice. If we choose to steal and are caught, we will likely be arrested, put in jail, humiliated publically, and will suffer the ramifications associated with breaking the law. We made the choice. But somehow, in the midst of the calamity that we caused, we cry out, "Why did you allow this, Lord?" We all do it. You know we do.

As it applies to the subject of this book, God is not to blame for not intervening in the abuse of animals. His permissive will invokes hope that mankind will willingly do right rather than wrong. So then it is not God who is to blame for his reluctance to intervene but rather our failure to do right.

I trust that satisfies any animosity toward God and the restraint He exercises.

Before we can move on to the more positive part of this chapter, one other side issue needs to be addressed; that of animal sacrifices reported in the Bible. It is apparent from the amount of mail I get on this topic that it is an important issue with many people who have pets. Many appear to hold God in contempt for not only allowing the practice to take place in Old Testament times, but proactively requiring it of Israel.

Satisfactorily explaining animal sacrifice is difficult when it is just a simple inquiry. When the question is framed in obvious bias (*"So explain to me how God could be so mean and unfeeling toward animals. I mean, I thought He was the God of love."*), the issue becomes very complicated. The response must address other underlying issues of bias or unbelief as well as answer the question. If I cannot satisfy the bias, it really doesn't matter what else I say.

For the record, I completely understand this bias. I was not always a Bible believer. I am not a Bible college drone who parrots everything taught by Bible-thumping pastors and professors. In fact, I was once an anti-Bible activist. I did not revere the Bible as God's Word. I did not hold it in very high esteem. Indeed, I once attempted to disprove it, but, in so doing, was exposed for the self-righteous fraud that I was.

Since that time, the Bible has passed every test I have put it through and has overwhelmed me with its insight and authority. It has proven itself accurate and timely and I now readily subordinate myself to it on any topic. .

So, I have no problem accepting animal sacrifices in the Old Testament without pointing an accusatory finger at God. I do not deny that, to modern-day understanding, sacrificing innocent animals as a sin offering is perceived as a barbaric, pagan act. But from God's perspective at that time, it was the only way He could offer reconciliation to those seeking it.

The Bible emphatically teaches that God is holy. He cannot sin. It is not in His nature. It is outside His ability to do. It is like you or I putting our hand in a raging fire. We cannot do it. It is against our self-preserving nature. Of course, there are exceptions to this rule for us. We might stupidly do it on a dare or a psychosis might be at play. But there is no exception for God. He is pure and holy and cannot change. He is immutable.

Moreover, He is not able to allow sin. His holy nature rejects it. He abhors it. Sin, He tells us, has no part in Heaven with Him. It sickens God to even be near it. This is an extremely difficult concept for humans to understand for we have been exposed progressively to more and more wickedness and have become increasingly more tolerant of it. But God is not tolerant. He abhors sin.

Sin condemns all humans to spiritual death. We are held accountable for our sins. We cannot rid ourselves of sin, therefore a price must be paid for it. The price that God demanded was innocent blood. He eventually sent His only begotten Son, Jesus, to be the ultimate innocent blood sacrifice for us. But until that time, He used the only possible alternative—animals.

Why animals? Simply, animals are sinless creatures. Their blood is innocent.

These innocent creatures used in sacrifice were a type of Christ, or a picture of how Jesus would become the ultimate sacrifice for mankind's sins as explained in the New Testament.

In fact, Jesus is referred to as the "Lamb of God" in John 1:29 which alludes or refers to the Old Testament practice of sacrificing lambs. Under the Old Testament dispensation of law, an animal's blood was the only solution or atonement for sin. But it was a temporary solution. Each year, atonement had to be made again by the priests. While the blood of animals was innocent, it was not holy. Only Christ the lamb of God's blood was both innocent and holy.

We wince at the demand of holy God for a blood sacrifice

for sin, but it was never His plan or desire for this to be. His creature, man, had sinned and separated himself from God, therefore God employed the only way possible for man to reconcile. Man sinned against God's will, but it was God's love and mercy that put into place the only way possible to appease His holiness, the sacrifice of innocent blood.

For those who cannot accept this method, for those who call Christianity a slaughterhouse religion, I can only tell you what the Bible says. You may not agree with what God had to do, but let me ask you what alternative did He have? Animal sacrifice was a temporary, symbolic substitute for the ultimate and perfect sacrifice that would be made by the coming Lamb of God, the Lord Jesus. By looking forward to Him and placing faith in the symbolic sacrifice, one was forgiven for their sin.

Having said all that, I am personally glad the shed blood of the Son of God is the propitiation for my sin and that the blood of animals is no longer needed. It doesn't make me feel better to know that the Son of God had to die for my sin, but it does help to know that God no longer requires a sacrifice, that the blood from His own lamb still applies to all who will accept Him and apply it to themselves.

The sum of the matter is this—animals suffer in this life. Some of the things that befall them at the hands of man are heinous and shameful. But again, that suffering is *at the hands of man* and not the will of God. One day, God will set all the crooked things straight, mend the hurt, and wipe away all tears. Until then, the blame remains ours and not God's.

Chapter 3

ANIMALS ARE ETERNAL SOULS

In two of my previous books, *Cold Noses at the Pearly Gates* and *Wagging Tails in Heaven*, animal lovers were provided with iron-clad evidence from the Bible that animals, like people, are eternal souls. Great care was taken to dismantle the commonly held erroneous view that animals are for this world only, that they simply cease to exist when they pass.

When challenged, few proponents of the commonly held school of thought can offer a reason for why they believe as they do. They cannot point to a Biblical passage or principle that supports their conclusion that animals are for this world only. When discussing their views, it becomes clear that what they believe is a reflection of what they heard a Seminary professor or former pastor say. No honest or earnest research into scripture was made to determine for themselves what the Bible teaches. They simply accepted what they had been taught by their professor, who had heard it from his professor, who had heard it from his professor, and so on.

It is dangerous for those who feel *called* to serve to accept without question all that is taught. The Bible teaches in Deuteronomy 13:14 that we should "Search out whether a thing is true. . . ." Professors and pastors are only men. They are not omniscient, nor are they immune from making errors. Too many cults and wayward ministries have sprung from the ideas of men that meant well, but who strayed from what God said in His Word.

Though this topic of animal souls is not an essential or major doctrine in terms of our Christian experience and mission, the precept of searching out a thing to be true or not still applies. No position should be taken on the matter until and unless one has thoroughly researched what God has to say about it in His Word. Discussions with literally thousands of fellow ministers from a wide variety of denominations has shown me that this is usually not the case.

The few who do actually attempt a scriptural explanation for their belief that animals are void of souls invariably point to the weak and theologically immature argument that claims God only breathed life into man. The passage they use as a basis for their erroneous belief is found in Genesis 2:7. "And the Lord God formed man of the dust of the ground, and breathed into his nostrils the breath of life; and man became a living soul."

It says only that God breathed life into man and he became a living soul. It does not exclude animals. They hypothesize however, that since it does not say He breathed life into the animals, they therefore cannot possibly have souls.

This argument is weak, but truly it is less than weak; it is anemic. There are so many flaws in this interpretation that I could probably fill this chapter with a response to those issues. However, I will limit myself to just the few major problems this theory presents.

I am sure readers caught the most obvious problem, but allow me to identify it anyway. It is the assumption that God breathed life into the man, but not the animals. Who then, did breathe life into the animals? We cannot deny that they live. We also cannot deny that God is the sole giver of life. No life exists except He animated it and caused it to be. It is safe to say then that God gave or breathed life into animals, even in the absence of words that tell us that He did. For anyone to say otherwise is to misrepresent the facts and ignore the tool of logic God gave us.

The second problem is if God only breathed life into the man, then who breathed life into the woman? If God did not breathe life into the woman, she, and therefore all women that follow her are creatures without souls. That conclusion is in gross conflict with what the Bible teaches—that each of us is a living soul.

One of the many rules of proper exegesis of scripture is that we should use the Bible to interpret the Bible. That is just a stuffy way of saying the Bible is never in conflict with itself. In other words, if the Bible addresses something in Genesis that is also mentioned in Matthew, each offering will support and not be in contrast with the other. The theory that God breathed a living soul only into men is in conflict with passages that teach otherwise and therefore fails that rule.

Finally, what of other men besides Adam? Following the strict interpretation assigned by the erroneous view that animals are void of souls, would not God have had to individually breathe life into each and every man who was born in order for them to have souls? But we are not told that God breathed life into other men, so can we then assume that He did not and therefore all men other than Adam are without souls?

Perhaps those who hold to this theory believe that the soul is transferrable from father to offspring like so many physical traits. If we imagine that it is, we have to make yet another incredible assumption and allowance. And we are then well on our way to teaching false doctrine.

The key to understanding this passage is in this word *soul*. The net result of God breathing life into Adam was not that He added a soul to that human being, but that He created a living soul and used the human being as a vessel for that soul. It is important to understand the distinction between having a soul and being a soul. We are not bodies with souls. Human beings are souls with bodies.

If you do a word study on the Hebrew word *nephesh* (soul), you will find that the word means *essence* or *life force*. So then, God breathed into Adam and he became a living essence. That essence is who he was, as our essence is who we are. The essence of a person is their consciousness, their mind, personality, cognitive process, emotions, and memories.

In my studies, it has become clear to me that the word *nephesh* is used in the Bible to address the essence of living animals as often as, if not more than, humans. And indeed it should. Animals possess cognitive skills, emotions, memories, and personalities. Often in the Bible, when discussing "the soul of every living thing," as in Job 12:10, for instance, God is speaking of both humans and animals.

Therefore, to declare that an animal has no soul is not only factually inaccurate—they do not *have a* soul, but *are* souls—it is also theologically and exegetically in error. The end verdict is clear. Animals are eternal creatures just like every other creature God created. Men and women live forever. Angels live forever, even those who rebelled against God will live forever. It only follows that God's other creatures— animals—also live forever. God is the giver of life, not the taker.

Cold Noses at the Pearly Gates and *Wagging Tails in Heaven* address many other questions asked after the passing of a beloved family pet. We will revisit a few of those issues in the following pages in order to introduce or reacquaint readers with foundational truths. This will allow us to discuss the reunion all pet people look forward to with clarity and assurance.

The evidence in scripture is clear; all life is from God and that life is eternal. Because animals are innocent creatures without sin, their eternal existence will be spent in the presence of their creator, or, if you prefer, Heaven. The Bible tells us that all of God's creation and creatures shall worship and praise Him there. I do not understand how anyone can be offended by the idea that animals are eternal creatures. God created them. God loves them. God says they are safe in His hands. It is just that simple.

Two other peripheral issues would be prudent to discuss to ensure there is no confusion regarding my position on the souls of animals and animal afterlife.

The first is the gospel message and its application to animals. I want to be absolutely clear where I stand on this issue; there is no application. Over the years, several of my contemporary ministers have accused me of preaching another gospel, as it were.

They have accused me of saying that animals can be born again. I have never said that, orally or in writing. I have in no way even hinted at or alluded to that possibility.

Some have seen the title of my first book, *Cold Noses at the Pearly Gates* and perhaps concluded that I was claiming animals could be part of the Kingdom of God the same way human beings can be, through salvation. This is absolutely a false assumption. I make clear distinction that humans and animals stand before God in different status. People are sinners in need of reconciliation with God. That is the gospel message, that God sent His son to die that he might be the means of our reconciliation with God.

Animals are innocent, sinless creatures. They have no need for reconciliation with God. They are "safe" in the hands of their creator. The gospel message was not for them, could not be understood by them, and could not be accepted by them. But they have a place in the kingdom, because God said they do. They are His creation and He loves them. How can this be so difficult for some to understand?

The second issue is closely related to the first, but with a bit of a twist. Recently, some of my early readers have taken it upon themselves to write books on the topic of animals and the afterlife. Some of those authors have taken theological liberties that are not theirs to take. Liberties, I might add, that are preposterous. Specifically, they have added the claim that the animals of Christians would be included in the rapture.

I am assuming you are aware of what I mean by *the rapture*. If not, a quick Google search will give you the details. Simply stated, it is the time the Bible speaks of when the Lord Jesus Christ will return to snatch true Christian believers away from the earth, both the living and the dead.

What these authors are saying is that when the Lord snatches away true believers, their animals will be snatched away with them. It is incredible that anyone who has any familiarity with the Bible and foundational Christian doctrine would make such a ridiculous claim. There is not one wisp or hint in scripture to support this outrageous notion.

The rapture is for believers and believers only. It is the whisking away, if you will, of the Bride of Christ (the body of believers) by the Bridegroom, the Lord Jesus Christ. He collects his living believers, reunites them with deceased believers from other times and relocates all to Heaven before the earth is subjected to the great seven year tribulation. No one else—no gentile or Jew, no angel or animal—is included in this event.

I honestly wish it were true that our animals were to accompany us in the rapture. It would be such a stress reliever for me to know my pets would not be left behind to fend for themselves, should the rapture occur in my lifetime. Unfortunately, that is not the case. The rapture is an exclusive event, pictured in illustration in the marriage parable of Matthew Chapter 22. For those who would have been a part of what they were not part of, the King (God) had them bound and cast out into outer darkness.

Though they already know the answer, I am often asked by fellow believers if there is any chance that I am wrong on my position on the rapture. There is not. But to help them cope, I offer guidance. It is not particularly insightful guidance. In fact, it is nothing more than stating the obvious, but surprisingly, it is not quite as obvious to them and it often proves to be a help.

For the benefit of any who may share their concerns, let me offer that same guidance. I do not mean for it to sound harsh, but sometimes it is difficult to speak the truth without it stinging. The Bible says "Faithful are the wounds of a friend," (Proverbs 27:6) meaning of course, that a friend will tell you the truth and the truth can wound, but it is meant to help, not to hurt. I offer these words only to help. *The pets of Christians will be left behind at the rapture, just as some family members and friends will be left behind.* The difference is that family and friends will be able to fend for themselves, but most of our pets will not.

Many animals will suffer and die. But animals suffer and die in huge numbers every day. It is the way of this woeful place we call Earth. But remember this. When they pass, they close their eyes to this world and immediately open them to the next. By virtue of their innocence, they are "safe" in their creator. Death for them is but a portal. It is a passing from life unto life. God holds the life of every creature in His wonderful, loving, eternal, almighty hands.

Knowing that they will be left behind, there are things we can do to ensure they are cared for in our absence. I used to carry a note around in my wallet to explain the rapture and ask whoever found the wallet to take care of my pets, offering them money that I'd left in a certain place in my house. I discontinued that practice when it finally occurred to me that if I lost my wallet before the rapture, I was inviting a break-in. I also realized I have family who are not believers and who would not be part of the rapture, either. I knew they would scoff at my asking them, but would undoubtedly care for my pets should I suddenly disappear.

I am sure you can come up with additional ideas on how to ensure the well-being of your pets in the event the rapture happens in your lifetime. In any event, remember that should the absolute worst case scenario develop and no one cares for them, they may briefly suffer, but the end of that suffering will be a new and better life and a grand reunion with you.

This might not be consoling to some of you, but I hope it will never actually be an issue for you in your lifetime

Chapter 4

WHAT IS THIS PLACE CALLED HEAVEN?

Heaven is a word that conjures up euphoric images of peace and tranquility for just about everyone who hears it. It is a positive word with absolutely no negative overtones. I have never heard anyone speak derogatorily about their concept of Heaven. All perceive it as a pleasant and desirable place to be. I have even heard self-proclaimed atheists use the word glowingly.

There is no shortage of ideas and concepts regarding this place. Invariably, every culture holds belief in some ultimate destination in the hereafter. Nirvana, Paradise, and Seventh Heaven are but a few of the labels used to identify Heaven. The list is long, but the ideas are largely the same. It is a place of rest or reward for those who are faithful to their respective beliefs.

For some, Hindus for example, the place of afterlife is temporary. Through *moksha* (a releasing of the soul) they believe they are reincarnated or literally reborn. For others, the hereafter is a permanent place. Still others believe there are multi-tiered levels where one works or earns their way to the most coveted level.

Ideas are usually religious in intent, but actually can be classified as being more cultish, metaphysical, or of the mythological cosmology nature. Further, each major camp of belief has minor subsets or splinter groups that adopt varying, and often contrasting beliefs with others of their faith.

I have not even scratched the surface of the diversity of beliefs. Nor do I want to. Here we are going to discuss the Heaven of the Bible—that place where the triune God of the Bible dwells. In doing so, we will reject all other claims regarding the afterlife. The Lord God is not only the one who created Heaven, but the one who speaks authoritatively about it in His Word. He assures us that all else is false and untrustworthy and I will proceed on that premise.

Of all the revelations we are given in the Bible, perhaps none has received more speculative attention than the place God calls Heaven. It seems most established authors of the religious or spiritual genre have taken a shot at writing something about it. Years ago, I saw a book written by a man who didn't believe Heaven existed, but wanted to write about it anyway.

At least he was honest. I have read many offerings that are not. One author stated emphatically that he knew there would be movie theaters in Heaven. Where do such thoughts come from? Where do they come up with such ridiculous notions?

The Bible is very clear on what it says about Heaven, but it really doesn't say that much. Believe me when I tell you if we discount the one-time heavenly events discussed in the book of the Revelation, the Bible doesn't say a lot about Heaven. In fact, if we were to pool all the Bible says on Heaven into one single digest, we might end up with four or five pages of single-spaced typing.

Amazingly, from this relatively miniscule amount of information, some authors have produced 500-page books describing Heaven in unbelievable detail. The descriptions largely lend themselves to gala events, parties, stellar fishing trips, and all the wonderful things they think Heaven will be. These are not factual but seem to be merely a projection of what the authors hope to find there.

That mind-set is representative of many, if not most people today; that Heaven is one big party or shindig. They have been told that Heaven is going to be everything their hearts desire. It is going to be everything we wish Earth could have been.

This message is delivered in the local churches and on a national level as well via television and radio. I have heard renowned preachers, men such as Billy Graham, go on record, saying, "Heaven will be whatever it has to be to make you happy." Where do they get this false notion from? As I read the Bible, and I have read and studied through it many, many times, I have never come across a passage that hints at such a concept.

Regardless, this seems to be the general consensus across denominational lines. Ask the average person what they think Heaven will be like, and almost without exception they will respond, "It is a place of happiness," or something to that effect. If queried further, they will elaborate on what it will take to make Heaven a happy place for them. One imagines he will be playing marathon golf, sporting an unearthly handicap. Another envisions endless championship fishing tournaments with himself as the star. Still others imagine unlimited charge accounts at enormous malls that never run out of stock and never close.

It is human nature to create in our minds our own personal

utopias. It is how we visualize and categorize our hopes. But human nature is exactly that part of us God does not want in His Heaven. Human nature is in contrast with God. In fact, in Romans Chapter 8 we are told that our flesh or carnality is nothing more than hatred against God. Actually, the rendering is that our flesh hates the things of God or Godly things.

Human nature is referred to in scripture by many names and all are seated in negative context. It is referred to as self, the flesh, the old man, and the old nature just to name a few. Our old nature is our sinful part, the selfish, self-centered and self-serving part. It is shown by God to be the cause of our sin and problems.

It is this human or earthly nature that lustfully imagines a customized Heaven and demands that Heaven will be what we want in order to make us happy. It is our self-centeredness that dictates what it would take for Heaven to be our personal utopia. Many believers are going to be surprised to find that Heaven is not at all what their flesh expected or wanted. Rather, they will find it is what God wants it to be.

So then, what is Heaven like? What does God have planned? The short and simple answer is I don't know. We are not given much detail on God's plans for eternity, except that we will spend much time around His throne fellowshipping with Him and undoubtedly, each other. Indeed, if we could quantify the heavenly experience in terms of time, most of our time will be spent worshipping and praising the Lord.

At the risk of shocking you further, let me say that I find the prospect of constant worship quite boring. I do not mean to be irreverent to the Lord, for certainly He is deserving of my eter-

nal praise, but somehow golf and fishing seem to resonate with
my excitement sensor more than a perpetual church service. If
worshipping twenty-four/seven was something that thrilled me,
why do I have so much trouble being faithful to church on Sun-
days when I get the sniffles? I am sure you can relate to this.

But that is just "me" talking, or my earthly flesh. The best my
old nature can imagine for Heaven is to concede to God cursory
time of praise and worship. The rest of the time available, my
old "me" nature wants for myself. In my present condition, though
regenerated and indwelt by the Holy Spirit, my old flesh still has
a modicum of control and influence in my thinking. Consequently, I often think in terms of what "I" want and what will
make "me" happy. And you do, too.

Fortunately, that will not be my condition when I enter Heaven. In I Corinthians 15:53 we are told "For this corruptible must
put on incorruption, and this mortal must put on immortality"
(KJV). . Right now, I am corruptible because of my flesh and
my desire is "me, me, me." But this verse tells me that when this
mortal shall put on immortality, it will also put on incorruption.
In effect, incorruption is not so much put on as corruption is put
off. Either way, I will be without my old nature when I leave this
world. Somehow, God will supernaturally and instantaneously
extract it from me and put it away.

Let me try to explain that better. When we accept the Lord,
essentially our salvation comes in three phases. First, immediately upon confessing Christ, we are saved from the *penalty* of
sin. Our sins are forgiven forever. There is no longer a penalty.
The wages of sin were paid by the Lord Jesus and our account
is paid in full.

As we live our Christian experience on Earth, we are saved from the *power* of sin. We are told that sin no longer has dominion (or control) over us (Romans 6:14). This is a quantitative term that means sin's influence is still present, but sin is not in control. We have the Holy Spirit within us teaching, convicting, and growing his fruit or attributes within us, helping us to turn from temptation.

Finally, when we pass or when the rapture occurs, we are saved from the presence of sin. This is huge. Sin will no longer be a part of us. The old man, the flesh, the old nature is supernaturally removed by God and put off. No longer is *self* important. No longer do we think in terms of "me" and "I."

In this new state where self is no longer the central focus, where sin has no presence, our new being will soar and excel. Without the old "me" to inhibit, worshipping God and praising His mighty works will be thrilling and exciting. We will hardly be able to contain the praise that pours from our lips as we fellowship with God. Golf, fishing, and all other leisure practices of the flesh will not even register on our "to do" lists. All we will want to do is sit in the presence of our Lord, overwhelmed with his majesty and wonder.

Think of that! Everything will be new and different. Think of what it will be like to not have sinful thoughts or be tempted. No more battles inside over right and wrong, for we will always desire to do right. Think of what it will be like to be truly content and happy.

Yes, Heaven will be a surprise for many, but it will be a pleasant surprise when we arrive there without our old nature. It will be a time unparalleled in our previous existence, where we no longer are influenced by the selfish flesh that housed our soul for so long.

Again, at this moment, while I am still housed in this flesh, the prospect of this type of Heaven is not overly appealing to me. It does not sound as exciting a place as Earth has been for me. I am ashamed to say that it actually sounds a bit stuffy and boring.

But if I make an effort to rise above my current secular existence for just a moment, if I allow my new nature to control my heart and mind, my soul is flooded with excitement and anticipation at this new life and world without the base things of Earth. Indeed, it will be a place a thousand-fold more than anything I could have hoped for or desired.

Chapter 5

WHAT IS HEAVEN LIKE?

As you might imagine, there are as many descriptions of Heaven as there are theories about what Heaven is. It is one religious topic almost everyone is willing to talk about. I presume that is because the thought of Heaven carries with it a very positive connotation and makes people feel good about the future.

Many ideas and concepts people have are so outrageously foreign to scripture, they border on ridiculous. One woman said God is a big ball of energy and Heaven is like an electric grid. Another said Heaven is like a big spiritual airport where all souls are cleared to land. Their ideas were kind of amusing, but not at all accurate.

There are those who claim to have visited Heaven via transcendental meditation, cosmic projection, or some other pseudo-spiritual means. They cannot tell you what it looked like, but when quoting a detail from the Bible, they are quick to say, "Oh yes, that's right. I saw that."

Pleeeeeeease! When I hear something like that I repeat what

I have said so many times before. "Pass the bread, the baloney has already been around."

So much New Age, easy-believism error is available to itching ears. You undoubtedly know that to be true, so I am not going to cover it here. A very wise old preacher once told me I would go crazy trying to correct every erroneous idea of God or the Bible that I encounter. He said that the best way to put error in its place was to just declare the truth. The truth, after all, will set us free.

As a Christian and Biblicist, I reject erroneous claims about Heaven, the "I visited there myself" claim in particular. The Bible teaches clearly, that short of the rapture, the only way to get to Heaven is to die. It also teaches that those who leave this life in this manner can never return. To claim otherwise, as some do, is to utterly and blatantly reject what God has told us.

When someone expresses, either orally or in writing, experiences that are at odds with scripture, a warning buzzer ought to go off in our heads. The Lord made it a special point to warn us in 2 John 1:7 that many deceivers would come into the world and that we needed to discern the counterfeit from the true. The litmus test is simple and works one hundred percent of the time. We hold religious and spiritual claims up to the light of the Word of God, which will either confirm it as true or expose it for the error that it is.

Please do not misunderstand what I am saying about those who deceive. I do not think all who claim to have "the truth" when it is in fact error, are intentionally trying to deceive. Quite the opposite is often true; they are themselves being deceived and are unwittingly and unintentionally deceiving others. Many believe that what they teach is the truth and they are earnestly trying to help others. So while I have a big problem with what they teach, I have no problem with their desire to do well for others. That notwithstanding, they still are, in effect, deceivers.

If that seems harsh, it is not meant to be. Sometimes there is no gentle way of stating the truth. If it is against what the Bible says, then it should be immediately suspect. Either the Bible is the sole trustworthy standard or it is not. Either it is all true and trustable or it is not true at all and completely untrustworthy. As one who first viewed the Bible as an ardent skeptic, but who now has studied its authenticity and embraces it as the preserved Word of the Living God, I choose to believe it all and think all others would do well to consider doing the same.

With that established and behind us, it is time to consider what the Bible has to say about this place called Heaven. To begin, let us establish first what Heaven is not. In light of some of the so-called television ministries on the "tube" these days, I think it prudent to take a moment to do so. Some very persuasive voices appear on television, some who are convincingly proclaiming the wrong gospel.

Heaven is not a pie in the sky country club as some claim. Christians were never told by the Lord to seek wealth. In fact, Jesus denounced riches as a major stumbling block to faith. I am sickened by the television preachers and speakers who spew out the nonsense of a financial gospel of abundance. The air waves are saturated with this new false gospel.

They shamelessly focus their sermons and presentations on the abundant life, telling viewers that God wants them to be affluent and well off . . . and they have just the plan to help you be obedient to God. They know how you can get your slice of that pie in the sky. All you have to do is send them the number of a major credit card and they will send you their books and videos and other paraphernalia to assure your success. How detestable that some will exploit people searching for truth and spiritual help for their own profit.

Am I being too judgmental? I don't think so. My guess is that I am being a lot less brutal than the Lord will be with them when they stand before Him to give an account of their preaching a false gospel of abundance and for misrepresenting Him. On the other hand, maybe there is something to what they say. After all, most of them are becoming wealthy, aren't they? Shame on them!

Moving on, allow me to give you a general snapshot of Heaven. I will follow that with a more detailed breakdown of some of the things God reveals to us about the place where He dwells. It's likely most who read this book will have previous knowledge of the Heaven of the Bible as a place of happiness, if not bliss and euphoria, and often referred to as a place of rest. They have been told that it is the place where God and His angels dwell and completely different from Earth and this life.

Theologians agree that Heaven is a spiritual place. I largely agree, but am not convinced that this is the whole story or best description. This conclusion is largely based on circumstantial evidence. We can't see Heaven. We cannot dial up the Hubble Telescope and focus in on it some billion light years away to see it. We cannot dial 411 and find a telephone contact number for someone living there.

So, since we cannot see it and cannot make contact with anyone who dwells there, we feel it can't be a physical place. It must be a spiritual locale, unreachable from a physical plane. For me, that doesn't work. Simply labeling Heaven as "spiritual" is not an adequate description. Rather, it is the easy way out.

There are other considerations relative to what we are told about this place, but we give them little or no thought because it is not a convenient time to do so. Heaven is far off in our minds and we still have a lot of living to do. Most people don't give Heaven much thought until they are in the winters of their lives.

Labeling it as a spiritual place, effectively removes it from their reality radar. This is probably why there are those who just do not care very much if it exists at all. They have postponed thinking about it for so long it has become relatively unimportant.

Don't misunderstand me. I am not rebelling against this commonly accepted position of Heaven being in the spiritual realm. I wholly agree with that assessment. I am merely saying I think there is more to the story. I am certain that while we on Earth view this place as being in a spiritual dimension, for those who presently dwell there, it is as physical a place to them as Earth was before their passing.

That is a fact easily ascertained from scripture. There, people who have passed from this life are physical beings, not spooky ghostly figures or unexplainable floating orbs. One good example is found in the book of Luke, Chapter 16. It is not a parable. The true life account takes place in Hades. The characters in the story are real people. They once were alive on Earth and are alive in the story. One of the characters in fact, is a well-known Old Testament figure, Abraham.

At the time of the story, Hades consisted of two independent compartments—Hades, where the unbelieving dead were placed, and Paradise, the peaceful place of rest for those of faith. Paradise no longer is a part of Hades as those who were there were relocated to Heaven upon the resurrection and ascension of Jesus Christ.

Briefly, Luke 16 tells us that there was an unbelieving rich man who was being tormented in the flames of Hades. Seeing Abraham afar off on the other side in Paradise, the man called out to him. He asked Abraham if Lazarus, a beggar the rich man had seen on Earth, might dip his finger in water and come to quench his thirst. Abraham advised the man that those in Paradise could not help those in Hades because of the physical barrier between them. There was no way for Abraham to send Lazarus because of the gulf between them.

Every element of this story speaks to the fact that the afterlife is a physical place. Those people had physical bodies. They felt physical thirst, pain, and emotions. They were limited in their ability to move by physical obstacles.

There are myriad scriptural examples like this one to support the fact that Heaven is, in and of itself, a physical place. How it can be spiritual and physical at the same time remains something to be understood, but God does not always explain things to us. Rather, He expects that we accept what He says as true. This is called faith—simply taking God at His word, without the empirical evidence science demands.

Science, which has evolved into a religion in its own right, rejects faith and seeks to explain everything. Sadly, science will often draw a conclusion and massage the facts to fit their preconceptions or bias. We cannot put the same faith in science we put in God, but that does not mean science is completely untrustworthy.

Science gets a lot of things right about the workings of the universe. It tells us our universe is three dimensional. It labels the dimensions Length (interval), Width (2D interval), and Height (cube). Some, like me, subscribe to a fourth dimension of Time, but the camps for and against still bicker over the legitimacy of this dimension. Then there is the fifth dimension, a group of great musicians popular in the 1960s and 70s. Okay, a poor attempt at humor. I beg your forgiveness.

Back to my point, which is that science operates and evaluates from a limited three or four dimensional perspective. Which number you subscribe to is not important here as I only wish to establish the limitations of the world we currently live in. Whether there are three dimensions or four does not change the fact that our awareness is limited to these few dimensions. Our perceptions are governed by the range of understanding that these dimensions allow us.

There are claims of others: alternate universes and multi-layered dimensions. Some physicists suggest that there are probably two dozen or more dimensions in the physical universe that we on Earth have either not been exposed to or cannot perceive. For a variety of reasons, I do not want to spend time on this, so if you are interested in learning more about this, a simple Google search for *hyperspace,* *wormholes,* or *quantum physics* will provide you with plenty of reading material on the subject.

As a side note, unless you are a shut-in, if you do not have a computer, you can visit your local library and use computers there for free. Many of these institutions have free basic computer courses to help you get over your apprehension of using this wonderful technology. If they do not, your local workforce center will have such courses. You may even be able to use their computers.

If you are a shut in, there are many programs where volunteers will come to your door with computer in hand to help you learn. There simply is no excuse for anyone to be computer illiterate these days. The World Wide Web gives you immediate access to more information than you can find in a dozen brick and mortar libraries.

Moving on, Heaven is most assuredly more than Earth in terms of dimensional diversity. After all, it is a spiritual realm, and, as we have seen, somehow physical as well. Heaven lacks the dimension of time, but potentially possesses many other perceptions. Perhaps the very absence of time is another dimension in and of itself. We simply do not know.

God also uses terms that do not seem to fit comfortably with our dimensional understanding. Terms such as *heavenlies* and *heavenly places* are two. Are these separate and distinct from Heaven itself or some sort of parallel dimension allowing the physical and spiritual to coexist? Who knows? We are not given enough information to know one way or the other. But whether or not the *heavenlies* are physical, spiritual, or something other than what our four dimensional understanding allows us to perceive or define, clearly there are greater physics at work in Heaven than on Earth.

The more we consider this possibility and the deeper we delve into scripture for answers, the more questions arise. For example, we know that God is real. He exists. If He didn't, we wouldn't.

But we are told emphatically that God is spirit and that no one can see Him. But if He exists, how is it that we cannot see Him? Everything we know about in this world, everything that exists, we are able to see. Sometimes it requires a microscope or a telescope to do so, but we can see it. So how can we not see God?

It gets even more complicated. We are also told (Hebrews 1:3) that Jesus is the express image of the Godhead, so that while we cannot see God the Father or God the Holy Spirit, we can see God the Son. We can see Jesus. We know this is true because so many people saw him in person in New Testament times and we have their record available to us as proof.

Here is the kicker for you scientific-minded folks (because believers have no problem accepting it). We are then told (John 10:30) that Jesus the Son and God the Father are one. How is it that we can see one and not the other? They are separate persons, but one and the same. How can that be? Again, the more questions we ask, the more questions we are faced with.

For believers, it isn't that this concept is too complicated to understand and accept, for faith always accepts what God says. It is just that in such matters, believers are like everyone else. We find it difficult to understand things outside and above our four dimensional thinking. I will be the first to admit that my finite mind gets confused when I think about higher things, things that transcend the knowledge of this world. For instance, if I allow myself to do so, I still get hung up on the age-old question *But where did God come from?*

For anyone who has not allowed themselves to take that question as far as their mind will take it, I encourage you to try. It is simply mind-boggling. The best I have been able to do is decide

that thinking it through is futile, that God must have had no beginning, just like the Bible tells us. How that is possible is not
for us to know, at least not yet.

Oh, the time I have spent on that one. I cannot tell you what
the answer is to that question. But I can tell you what the process
and result of contemplating it is—a headache, a struggle with
one's faith, and finally a feeling of utter awe as I realized the unfathomable greatness of God. Sometimes there just are no answers.

Another example of our dimensional consciousness deficit would
be the record of the book of the Revelation. As the book unfolds,
we are not only referred back to many Old Testament prophecies, but the emphasis and location of what we are reading about
continuously switches back and forth from Heaven to Earth and
from Earth to Heaven. In some passages, time is suspended temporarily and we catch glimpses of future things that will yet come
to pass.

We are given vivid descriptions of creatures we have not seen
on Earth, and are exposed to causes and effects we have not experienced in our physical world. The problem is not that what
is said is hard to accept and understand, but rather that we are
unfamiliar with these things and cannot readily relate to what is
being said.

Suffice it to say the two realms, spiritual and physical, each
created by God, are separate one from the other . . . and yet in
Heaven they interact in harmony. In fact, they can overlap and
interact whenever God wills them to.

Take for example the transfiguration, an event recorded in the
gospels that most people are familiar with. Jesus took his disci-

ples up into a high mountain and was transfigured before them. As the disciples looked on, Jesus stepped out of the physical world and into the spiritual. His robe turned exceedingly white and he clearly was in the spirit as he communed with Elijah and Moses from the afterlife.

He was transfigured from a physical being to a spiritual being right before their eyes. And then, having completed his business with them, he stepped back into the physical world and rejoined his earthly followers. His disciples who witnessed this were astonished to the point of fear. They had been exposed to something unfamiliar to them. They knew what they saw, but did not understand it.

Whatever this place called Heaven is, believers can be assured of this one thing. Jesus said, "In my father's house are many mansions; if it were not so, I would have told you. I go to prepare a place for you" (John 14:2). We may not understand it all now, but because that place is being prepared for us, we can rest assured God will instill us with understanding when the time comes.

Now, let us look at the details we are given about Heaven. I have organized this section into simple subcategories in order to make them easier to digest.

THE DIMENSIONS OF HEAVEN

Though Heaven may indeed be comprised of many more dimensions than we are accustomed to in this life, we are obliged to define it using the limited perceptions available to us. Undoubtedly our best efforts will be inadequate and fall far short of the mark they ought to hit, but we are without alternatives in this matter. We can only use the cognitive skills and tools of perception given to us in this life.

Part of my research for this book included a canvassing of appropriate Christian websites to see what others were saying about the place the Bible calls Heaven. I was surprised and quite concerned to find that an extraordinary number of people are confused even with what Heaven we are referring to. I would like to try my best to remove that confusion.

I think it is expedient for us to know what Heaven we are talking about. There is more than one that we are told about in the Bible. In fact, there are three. First, there is the immediate atmosphere surrounding the Earth; second, the universe beyond Earth's atmosphere; and third, the place where God dwells.

This third place is the place we traditionally call Heaven, or the final place of rest for believers. However, there are actually two such places independently mentioned in scripture. The present Heaven is where God, His angels, and saints (believers) reside. One day, He will create the new Heaven or New Jerusalem (Revelation, Chapter 21).

Some get confused about the New Jerusalem. They feel it is a temporary abode for the redeemed and that the "New Heaven" mentioned earlier in Chapter 21 of the Revelation will be something God creates later as our actual eternal home. Careful reading of that passage shows that this is not the case. The second verse of the chapter labels this New Heaven as the Holy City, the New Jerusalem. It will be our eternal home, but we will not occupy that beautiful city until after the Great Tribulation and final millennium, which is 1,007 years from whenever the rapture occurs.

The New Jerusalem, which is also known as the Tabernacle of God, the Heavenly Jerusalem, the City of God, the Holy City, and the Celestial City will literally be Heaven on Earth. Perhaps Heaven *near* Earth is a more accurate description as we are told that it will sit literally in the sky above Earth.

I understand this sounds like something from a fairy tale. The first time I heard this, that was exactly the thought I had. We can attribute that reaction to our limited earthly experiences. Having studied the topic for so many years, I know God means exactly what He said. This city will sit in the clouds.

In Heaven, those who have passed from this world to that place, with exposure to heightened dimensions and perceptions, undoubtedly have no problem viewing this prophecy with great "know so" anticipation. We on Earth must accept it by faith.

I assure you that the New Jerusalem will be created by God. It will be very little like its namesake, the original Jerusalem with us now. It will be populated by believers only. It will house the church, the Bride of Christ, as we are told in Revelation 21:9-10.

*And there came unto me one of the seven angels
which had the seven vials full of the seven last
plagues, and talked with me, saying Come hither, I
will show thee the bride, the Lamb's wife. And he
carried me away in the spirit to a great and high
mountain, and showed me that great city, the holy
Jerusalem, descending out of heaven from God.*

Undoubtedly the population of this holy city will include the redeemed Jews and gentiles of the pregospel dispensations, as evidenced by the mention later in the chapter of individual tribal stones in the city's adornment. But primarily, it is the city made by the Bridegroom (Jesus) for his bride (the church). It is the fulfillment of His promise in John 14:2 to ". . . go and prepare a place . . . and receive you unto myself."

Not only is the promise of Jesus to his bride fulfilled in the delivering of this holy New Jerusalem, but it also fulfills or completes the Old Testament example or type that we saw in the Temple where God dwelled with His people as Shekinah glory, which loosely translated means *dwelling glory*, or God's glory dwelling with His people. That is why the New Jerusalem is also called the Tabernacle of God.

This holy city will be a hundred times the size of the original city of Jerusalem on Earth at this moment. Roughly, the New Jerusalem's three-dimensional measurements will be 1,500 miles long, 1,500 miles wide and 1,500 miles high—a cube. It will cover 2,250,000 square miles, roughly one quarter the size of the contiguous United States.

Artists' conceptions of this cubed city on the Internet look strangely similar to the Borg cubes we were introduced to in several of the *Star Trek* offerings. Perhaps there will be some similarity in general shape, but undoubtedly the similarities end there. It will be a breathtaking city void of any of the ills we see in earthly cities or the industrialized wasteland on the imaginary Borg cubes.

The streets shall be paved with transparent gold in the purest and most precious form. The gates and other internal structures will be decorated with precious stones that will project a regal brilliance. The city will dazzle onlookers and draw eternal praise to the architect who designed and prepared it.

Much more could be said about the New Jerusalem, but I think it is important to move on, describing the present Heaven—where we go when we die and where our reunions will take place.

So how can we define Heaven? What are its dimensions? Is it a planet like Earth or just an existence on a spiritual plane? If it is spiritual and physical, as we have surmised, the substance of it will have to be large enough to fit everyone who is or who will be there. How big is that?

All good questions to be sure.

The actual size of the present Heaven is unknown. We are not given any specific information, however, I think it is safe to make an assumption regarding the size. And before I do so, let me say, "Yes, I know the old joke about what assuming is." I don't know what knucklehead came up with that cliché joke, but there is nothing wrong with making an assumption based on the facts available. An assumption is a good guess, nothing more. God has given us logic and the ability to deduce. Drawing conclusions is a necessary and natural function.

And so, I am assuming, based on the facts available, that Heaven must be a rather huge place. Perhaps it is not as large as the New Jerusalem will be, but surely it is a grand place on every possible level. Let's not forget the inhabitants are the redeemed (those who put their trust in God) from every dispensation of mankind's history. The total population could easily number into the billions.

Regardless of size, the regal décor will undoubtedly reflect the majesty of the Most High. Kings on Earth spared no expense to ensure that they were surrounded with the most beautiful and breathtaking trimmings. God the Father will undoubtedly decorate the home of his only begotten Son's bride, in never-before-seen splendor.

Accommodations for those who are called after his Son's name (Christians) will not be shabby. God is not going to have tenement housing. Our presence with Him for all eternity is a big deal to Him. It seems to me that our reunion with God is looked upon with as much joyous anticipation on His part as it is on ours. So when He said He would prepare a place for us, irrespective of whether in the current Heaven or New Jerusalem, I am sure He has spared no luxury.

God does not do anything small. We read in Exodus that He parted the Red Sea for the chosen people. He didn't send a boat or make them walk around. He did it purposeful and in a big way. In Genesis, He rained fire down on Sodom and Gomorrah. He didn't send eviction notices or just turn the lights off. It was a spectacularly big event. When He created the Earth, He didn't let it stand alone in space. He decorated the sky around it in a very big way with trillions of other stars and planets.

Trillions? Really . . . trillions? Is that a bit of an exaggeration? Actually, when I have spare time, I enjoy sitting alone while I quietly ponder the greatness and wonder of God's creation,

I used to lay awake in bed for hours thinking about the vast reaches of what we call "outer space." I mentioned Star Trek earlier. I am not ashamed to say that I am a Trekkie. I loved the adventure in television shows like Star Trek. Hollywood doesn't do much right, but the picturesque space scenery that they came up with in that series seemed so real and so close to what I imagined, that it was thrilling to watch. As I said, I would lay awake for hours in bed, just thinking about what God made and wondering why He made it as vast as it is. I sit on the porch or take walks gazing upward into the heavens to indulge my passion. Thus far I haven't fallen asleep during a walk, but admittedly, I have struggled occasionally with staying conscious while sitting on the shady porch on a warm summer day.

God's creation is simply astonishing. The more I contemplate and measure in my mind what God has made, the more I am in awe. I think of the literally trillions of planets and stars He created from nothingness and it throws my mind into overdrive trying to comprehend it all. He used no raw materials; He simply willed them to be and they were. How is power like that possible?

Some of these planets are thousands of times the size of Earth. What enormous masses God made by simply willing them into existence. When I compare His vast and awesome power to my pipsqueak abilities, I am greatly humbled. God is wonderfully incredible.

I realize I am on a rabbit trail at the moment and I should get back to describing Heaven, but in my mind, heralding God's greatness is appropriate at any time and it is one of my weaknesses. So I ask for your forgiveness for this detour and your indulgence for just a moment. I will be brief and we will return to the description of Heaven in just a moment.

I mentioned trillions of planets and stars earlier and I know that most readers probably balked at that number, thinking I was exaggerating. I understand. We often use exaggerated numbers to make a point (i.e., *"If I have told you once, I have told you a million times . . .*"). But I am not exaggerating. If anything, I have understated the facts. Let me explain.

I not only like to sit and contemplate God's handiwork we call the universe, but I do a lot of online reading and research, as well. Drawing on information anyone can find on some of the better known websites about the things of the universe (www.nasa. gov, www.universetoday.com), I have come upon some amazing facts and tidbits of information.

I think you will find them interesting as well, so I want to share them. I hope they have the same impact on you as they did on me. I hope they provoke you to sit and consider the greatness of God through the witness of His awesome and extraordinary creation. He certainly deserves it.

To keep this simple, I am going to talk in oversimplified terms and avoid scientific terminology. The word *science* may confer that an unwavering set of rules are at work, but in truth, most major hypotheses and regimens have two or more camps of thought associated with them. One group of scientists will think one way; another group or groups think an entirely different way. Scientific truth is not always as concrete as we may think.

Global warming is a good example of this. With the global warming theory a wide spectrum of "truths," pro and con, are being forced upon the public. Both sides of the scientific argument are so vehemently opposed to the other's point of view they have purposely let their differences bleed over into the public arena of politics as they seek to validate their positions. When scientists use politics to sway public opinion, they have lost their objectivity and quite possibly their credibility.

I have found this same imbalance at work when it comes to the universe, in terms of its dimensions and components, though it has not yet become political. As you read through this section of this chapter, please keep in mind that I have no ulterior political agenda. I merely am trying to celebrate the awesomeness of God through His amazing creation.

Science has divided up our universe into chunks of space called quadrants, which comes from the root word *quarters*. Quadrants are usually three dimensional measured spaces of fixed sizes. They are a certain length, a certain width, and a certain height. It is impossible to affix such measurements to our universe because we do not know the actual size. We have not been able to see the scope of it. Indeed, some hold that it is endless. Irrespective of that, all at least agree that it is much larger than what we have been able to see.

On top of that, science has established (and all seem to agree) that the universe is expanding and therefore in a state of flux. Measuring an expanding universe would be akin to changing the tire on a moving vehicle, so we will allow that the universal quadrants are big and getting bigger.

Within those quadrants, measurement changes from chunks of size to numbers. Specifically, the number of stars and planets in a group is measured. In each quadrant, the smallest measurement group is called a solar system. In our quadrant, Earth is in a solar system that consists of nine planets (eight if you discount Pluto as some scientists suggest), their moons, and the sun.

The next higher measurement, which is again termed *quadrant* is actually a small designated portion of space within the larger quadrant or quarter of the universe and one of four parts of a galaxy. Earth and our solar system is part of the galaxy called the Milky Way.

Now this is where it starts getting exciting. It is estimated there are between 300 and 400 billion stars and planets in the Milky Way galaxy. Wow, that is a lot of planets, is it not? That is amazing. And it is amazing someone actually counted them all. Well actually, most of the counting work was done by computers interpreting photographs and other data. It is hard to grasp such a large number, so let me use an illustration that will put this in a perspective we can understand more clearly.

The common marble is a spherical shape, roughly the same diameter as a dime. I did some rough math and discovered it would take approximately 400 billion marbles to fill a National Football League stadium. That is a lot of marbles, and they represent a lot of planets. But hold on, I am not finished with this illustration. There is even more to consider. The Milky Way is but one galaxy. Experts estimate there are at least 200 billion other galaxies out there just like our Milky Way. Yes, I said billions with a *b*.

Continuing with our illustration, after we complete our task of filling one NFL stadium with marbles to represent the planets and stars in one galaxy, in order to show how many stars and planets there are in the remaining galaxies, we will have to fill another 200 billion stadiums with marbles. For the record, the surface of the Earth is not sufficient in size to hold that many stadiums. Surely that revelation must shock you.

You can check my math if you like. In fact, I wish you would, because the number is so absolutely incredible I know it will bowl you over as it has me. But you will have to do it long hand as I did. My calculator would not compute a number this large. The number of planets and stars in the universe totals eighty sextillion. Sextillion comes after quintillion, which comes after quadrillion, which comes after trillion. It is an unfathomable number that looks like this numerically: 80,000,000,000,000,000,000,000.

But wait; I am not done yet. These estimates are purposely low-balled by scientists. A super computer in Germany fixes the number at nearly twice that and an even more current study doubles that number, fixing the amount at 300 sextillion planets and stars. That would put the total into the septillions—specifically 3 trillion times 100 billion. That number is so extraordinary it is seldom used in any venue. Consequently, it was difficult for me to research and discover the appropriate word to use.

There is yet one other factor to add to the mix. One hundred years ago our current technology would have been considered extraordinary, perhaps even impossible or supernatural, especially given folks' predisposition to superstition way back then. But as superior as it is, technology still has limitations. We can see just so far into the universe. That was the reason Hubble was built and launched, so we could see farther.

Even with the Hubble's vastly superior reach, estimates are that we have not even seen half of what is out there, and quite possibly a whole lot less than that. We are only able to see shadows and wavy anomalies that most certainly would prove to be other galaxies with billions of additional stars and planets.

Let me attempt another crude illustration to put these extraordinary numbers into a scenario most of us can understand. Help me out on this please. Take a regular 8½ x 11 inch sheet of bond paper and place it on a table.

Tap the end of a ball point pen or a pencil on the paper so it makes a small dot. Let that dot represent one planet. Repeat that action over and over again as rapidly as you can, making as many independent dots on the sheet of paper as you can. When you are done, count the total dots (or keep track as you are making them).

For your convenience, I have already completed this task. The total I came up with before the dots began overlapping each other was approximately 50,000. Okay, I lost count a couple of times, but I wasn't about to start over. But my estimate is within a 50-dot error factor and that's not too bad. So, the sheet represents 50,000 planets and stars, give or take 50.

I did not make any allowance for differing sizes. Had I done so, the actual amount of dots would have been considerably less, so recognize that we are erring on the conservative side of this illustration. The end result will again be a low-ball figure.

Assume it is humanly possible to make a sufficient number of copies of this sheet so when laid side by side they cover the length, width, and sides of the Great Wall of China, leaving no portion of the wall exposed.

Allowing that the wall is nearly four thousand miles long, has an average height of twenty-two feet on each side, with a walkway approximately sixteen feet across, you would need to make an extraordinary number of copies of your sheet in order to cover the wall. In fact, you will need to make a little over one trillion copies. If you get it in your noggin to actually perform this experiment, you are going to make some local printing vendor very, very happy.

You would also make an overseas freight and shipping company ecstatic as you would need a fleet of approximately two hundred large cargo vessels to transport the more than four million tons of paper. Then, upon docking in China, you would need more laborers to carry the paper than were actually needed to build the Great Wall.

The numbers are extraordinary. Well hold on to your hat, because that is not the final step in our illustration. Now that you have covered the Great Wall completely, your one trillion sheets of fifty thousand planets each represent only a very small portion of the total number of planets in the known universe.

You are going to have to repeat that whole process 80 million more times. Then, and only then, will you have a dot representing every planet and star in the known universe. Are you getting the picture of just how wondrously amazing God and His creation are?

All things considered, the implications are staggering. Earth is but a single grain of sand on a one hundred mile long beach, with all the other grains representing other planets or stars. The beach is only one hundred yards wide, but we might find that the unseen, underwater part of the beach is many times larger than the actual beach we see. The same is probably true with the universe. When our technology is advanced enough to see much farther than we do now, we might find that the rough quadrants may need to be vastly expanded.

The question "Why did God make the universe so huge, with so many planets and stars?" could be asked. The only possible answer is that God doesn't do things in a small way. He desires to be worshipped and praised by His creation and it would be an unreasonable expectation if He did not display His great power and ability.

When taking in the immensity and wonder of His creation, how can anyone not pause to consider with awe the power of Almighty God? It is not just awesome and unbelievable; it is silencing. It overwhelms and mutes the most ardent skeptic. It numbs the keenest minds.

At His whim (I am not saying God is whimsical) He brought this vast universe, with trillions of planets and stars into existence. And with that same unfathomable power, He holds it all together—every galaxy, every solar system, every planet, every star, every moon, every mountain, every stone, every molecule and atom. It is pretty safe to assume that when it comes to size, He did not cut corners in Heaven.

THE BEAUTY OF HEAVEN

We all have a picture in our minds of what Heaven may look like. Without exception, I am confident this picture is one of beauty. After all, we are talking about Heaven, perhaps the only topic in the history of mankind always referred to and referenced in a positive light. Well, maybe we can include the cuteness of babies, puppies, and kittens in that exclusive category.

Whether we concocted that picture on our own or were influenced by others to adopt it really doesn't matter. That does not detract from the positive perception we have. Still, it would be prudent for us to know the facts. Where better to find those facts than with the one who designed, built, and lives in this beautiful place?

In I Corinthians 2:9 God tells us "But as it is written, eye has not seen, nor ear heard, neither has entered into the heart of man, the things which God has prepared for them that love him."

God only hints at the beauty of Heaven, but He does so in a very poetic and intimate way. Embodied in the glimpse He gives us is an assurance of the love He has for us. In the book of John, the Lord told us before He departed that He was going to prepare a place for us, and in I Corinthians He alludes to the sheer wonder and beauty of that place.

But He guards His words so as not to give away too much detail—almost as if He doesn't want to spoil the surprise He has for us. And isn't that how you act when you love someone and want them to be happy with what you have done for them? You cover their eyes and guide them into another room where you have that beautiful cake or present waiting for them.

There is also a good probability that if God were to reveal the details of Heaven to us, we would not be able to wrap our finite minds around them. When the Apostle John saw the Lord Jesus in his glory in Heaven (Revelation 1:17), he fell down as a dead man. The sight was too much for him to absorb. Throughout scripture are similar examples of this sort of reaction to exposure to infinite things while still in finite flesh.

The Apostles John and Paul reported that they were restrained, or otherwise supernaturally prevented, from sharing some of what they were told by the Lord or angels. It is likely that what they were told could not be easily understood. Indeed, they themselves struggled with it.

Not knowing every minute detail about this destination called Heaven should not be a discouragement for us. If we book a cruise, we want the details about our destination. We want to know something about the place we are going to and what kind of fun we can expect to have there. That allows anticipation and excitement to build.

For destination Heaven, however, Jesus told us not to worry. He would ensure it was ready for us and that it would be a place better than any other place that has ever existed. For us, excitement and anticipation is present from the moment of salvation and nurtured from within by the Holy Spirit who indwells us. If Christians were any more excited about going to Heaven, people would think we were suicidal and that is not at all the message the Lord wants us to send.

Even conceding that there are not a lot of details provided, there is much to glean from our text. First, we are told ". . . eye has not seen . . ." Think of what this means. No living human has ever seen anything as beautiful and wonderful as Heaven.

I grew up in Hawaii. The Aloha state is undoubtedly one of the most beautiful places on Earth. The ma uka (mountains), aina (land), and kai (ocean) combine with the constant blue sky to enchant all onlookers. Our scenery, particularly on islands other than Oahu where overcrowding and expanding industry has robbed the island of much of the beauty that once existed, is simply breathtaking.

The beaches of the islands come in a variety of colors—white, tan, black, and red, for example. Often, these beaches leave an indelible impression on visitors and on the mainland, they become walking advertisements for Hawaiian tourism. It is not uncommon for first time visitors to make a special point to ask tour guides to show them these beaches.

Over three thousand species of birds serenade those who spend time outdoors, even at the tables of outdoor restaurants, where they will "perform" for a few crumbs of bread. Whether outdoors or in, one cannot mistake the fragrant bouquet of our vast variety of flowering plants, wafting everywhere on the gentle trade winds.

The fragrance of night blooming flowers, which we locals call Mock Orange or Night-Blooming Cereus, coupled with a full moon shining through the soft Hawaiian clouds intoxicates strolling lovers. Many a proposal has been generated beneath the enchanting Hawaiian moon while under the influence of that heavenly fragrance.

Beautiful as Hawaii is, eyes have seen it. Eyes have seen Angel Falls. Eyes have seen the Napa foothills in California. Eyes have seen the White Cliffs of Dover. But eyes have never seen anything like the beauty God has prepared in Heaven for those who love Him. Earth's beauty spots are memorable, but they will pale in our memories when we behold the splendorous beauty of Heaven.

Perhaps the most beautiful feature of Heaven will be the Lord Jesus Christ in all of his majesty. He is the beautiful bridegroom in the Song of Solomon, the lily of the valley, and the light of the world. Surely all of Heaven will be aglow with His beauty.

This first part of our passage ". . . eye has not seen . . ." causes me to think fondly of the late Frances Van Alstyne, blind hymn writer and wonderful Christian woman. You may recognize her better by her adopted name of Fanny Crosby.

Fanny was a persevering spirit. Despite her challenging condition, she wrote more than eight thousand Christian hymns that have been sung by literally hundreds of millions of voices. And that is probably an understatement. Some like "Blessed Assurance" and "Pass Me Not Oh Gentle Savior," I, like so many other millions of believers, have sung a thousand times myself.

Despite her many noteworthy accomplishments, the thing I remember best from Fanny's biography was an answer she gave when asked the question, *If you could change anything in your life, what would it be?* Obviously, most of us would answer, *"That I could see!"*

Surprisingly, that was not Fanny's response. Her answer was that she wished she had been blind from birth. That may seem like a strange response from someone who was blind most of her life, but I assure you that it was a well-considered answer.

Fanny explained that she had been born with sight, but an eye ailment had taken her vision before she was two months of age. Though she could not remember seeing anyone's face in that early part of her life, she was sure that she had. It was reasonable to assume that she had seen her mother and father's faces, at the very least.

Her love and devotion for the Lord Jesus was so perfectly selfless that if she could have changed anything in her earthly life, it would have been that the first face she ever saw in her existence would be the face of Jesus. Because she was a deliberate and honest woman, I am sure she meant every word.

I like it when I know the wishes of someone have come true. I especially like it when the wishes come true for someone who was born into this life with a challenging condition. Since 1915, Fanny's wish has been coming true as she has been enjoying that face she so longed to see.

The next portion of I Corinthians 2:9 says ". . . nor ear heard . . ." Primarily, this means that no human being has ever been able to come back from the dead and report on the beauty and wonder of the Heaven God has prepared for us. The Lord repeatedly makes brief mention of the place, but again, never with great detail.

We know it is beautiful because we take the Lord at his word. We also yield to his assessment that we have not seen or heard of a more beautiful place, because He alone has experience in both worlds and is therefore the only one qualified to make such a comparison.

I believe this portion of the verse also speaks to our having never heard the beautiful sounds and songs of Heaven. We know there will be a choir there, but our only experience with choirs on Earth may not allow us to absorb and appreciate the perfect blend of melody and harmony in Heaven. I do not mean to be cruel, but I have heard some choirs that were nothing to write home and tell mother about, especially after my voice was added.

Whatever awaits us, I am certain our ears are in for a treat. Music on Earth is inspirational and moving. In Heaven it will undoubtedly take on new dimensions that will live up to the claim of this verse.

My wife has always been one of the premier soloists at the various churches we have belonged to as we moved around the country. Her Polynesian voice is typically sweet and pure. On top of that, she is musically inclined and gifted. I know, because as I hinted earlier, I am not. People who cannot sing usually can appreciate and single out people who can. I am sure you know what I mean.

Now don't misunderstand. I sing a wonderful song, keeping the correct tempo and timing without flaw . . . at least in my head. But somewhere between my mind and my vocal cords, it all comes apart. Consequently, what comes out is far from what is supposed to come out.

The good thing is that I recognize my musical shortcomings. I am not deluded about my vocal abilities as are so many on one American talent show. My goodness, I sing better than many of those contestants, but I know that I am not very good. Don't they have people in their lives who care about them and could keep them from being humiliated on national television?

All kidding aside, I do have a fair voice. I just have difficulty getting the tune right. When I get stuck on flats and sharps, my wife walks me through it. She is very patient; sometimes it takes thirty or forty attempts before I finally have it right and can lock it into my memory.

But she has no such problem. Notes come to her easily. She is very talented. I have never heard her hit a sour note in the hundreds of times I have heard her sing. Yes, I know I am tone deaf and some are thinking maybe that is why she sounds so good to me, but my problem is producing a good tune, not hearing and appreciating one. I am very good at that. Besides, I have the rest of the church as additional proof. She is well loved wherever she ministers.

What I wanted to say about her singing though is more about her approach than her delivery. She holds sacred music sacred. She chooses reverently worded and arranged music and sings them in reverential style. Her attitude is to focus the listener's attention on the things of God and to bring glory to Him, not herself.

In fact, whenever we would minister at other churches for vacationing pastors, the people there, who were not aware of her humble spirit, would often enthusiastically applaud her performance. If they knew her, they would know that showing her praise like that bothered her greatly.

My point is her reverent approach and style ensures as sweet a presentation as any earthly song can get, but it still falls far short of what we will find on that distant shore of Heaven. The music there will be more beautiful than any classical piece any ear has ever heard. It will be sweeter, loftier, and far more inspiring than any sound we have on Earth.

Moving on to the final part of the passage we are going to discuss ".... neither has entered in to the heart of man ...," what does that mean exactly? It simply speaks to our imagination. We are assured that the wonder and beauty of Heaven is so far above anything seen on Earth, our minds cannot conjure up anything that resembles it. Not with creative thinking, not during a daydream, not even in our sleep as we dream. We cannot imagine what a beautiful place Heaven will be.

Oh truly, our imagination can create new thoughts and images. There is almost no limitation as to what an active, vivid mind can dream up. It does have one big limitation, however. It can only draw upon the experiences of this Earth-locked life that we live and the few things not of this world that God chooses to disclose to us in His Word.

Our experiences are governed by our senses; what we have seen, touched, heard, tasted and smelled. Since our imagination can only draw upon the three or four dimensional experiences we have had, perception of a multi-dimensional Heaven is outside our capacity. We may think our ideas are wild, insightful, and even revolutionary, but God dedicated an entire Bible book to remind us that "There is nothing new under the sun. . . ."

We are finite, limited beings. Our imaginations are limited. Not only have we never seen or heard of anything like the beauty of Heaven, if we deliberately attempted to stretch our imagination to that high level, our faculties would fail us.

For those of us who have lost pets, knowing they are in that place of beauty right now, at this very moment, enjoying all God has prepared for us should thrill our souls. They and all who have passed to Heaven have a huge advantage over us who are still on Earth—they have seen. They have heard. And their hearts are able to comprehend it all.

THE WONDER OF HEAVEN

Along with the beauty of Heaven, I have mentioned the wonder of that place. Wonder is the unexpected impact or surprise someone or something has upon us. It is the spectacle or wonder of a thing that puts us in awe.

I have no doubt but that we will literally *gasp* at the wonder and spectacle of Heaven one day. We have all had such reactions to various stimuli on Earth; picturesque scenery, the girl or boy we love dressed to the hilt, or seeing someone we love who we haven't seen in years. In Revelation 8:1 we are told

And when he had opened the seventh seal,
there was silence in Heaven about the space of
half an hour.

When the seventh seal was opened, it released or initiated the seven trumpet judgments of the Great Tribulation period. These judgments against the Earth will be so severe that all God's host will hold their silence in awe for about half an hour at the wonder of it.

Two important points are to be made here. First, referring to this passage was intended to be an example of how the things God does can impact us. One should not think the wonder of Heaven will include such negative stimuli as this scene during the Great Tribulation period. The wonder in Heaven will be uplifting, thrilling, and positive. But I thought this passage would be a good example of what wonder there is in the things that God does.

Second, the reference to a measurement of time is to give us a reference we can understand and relate to. In no way does this suggest that time exists in Heaven. It does not, as we shall see in the next segment below. We are merely being told heavenly things with earthly applications, using earthly measurement tools to facilitate our understanding.

Heaven will be a place of wonder at all levels. Even the fact that there is no measurement or compartmentalization of time will be something we marvel at for a very long time (pardon the pun).

TIME WILL BE NO MORE

One of the foundational aspects of our earthly life is the dimension of time. Without time, life would be disorganized and inefficient. There would be mass confusion. No one would know when to do this or that or be here or there. We live by routine; rising at a certain time, working during certain hours, taking meals at roughly the same times each day, playing and sleeping habitually at the same hour. We work, play, and operate within the confines of measurements of time. We segment our lives into terms of minutes, hours, days, weeks, months, and years.

Our perceptions are dependent upon these chunks of time. We know someone is old by the number of years they have lived. We do not have to see their hair turning gray or age spots developing. All we need is to know their number of years. We know how far we can jog by the allotted time we can dedicate to the task. We feel fatigued, usually not because we have not slept long enough, but rather because we are aware that we have not slept the recommended number of hours.

In Heaven, that will all be behind us and gone forever. Time is of Earth. Time is the instrument that implements cause and effect, which is the engine of our present existence. We eat (effect) because we are hungry (cause). We drink because we thirst. Our needs are the cause and what we do to satisfy those needs is the effect.

In Heaven cause and effect, and time will be no more. God exists outside time and space and all that is associated with them. We will exist with God, who will already have provided for all our needs, including needs we will not even be aware of.

Let me shift gears here to try to start bringing this chapter to a close. Occasionally a reader will contact me to ask me if I think their pets miss them. I appreciate that they assign me such a lofty ability of insight and place such confidence in my opinion, but sometimes it is recognition I do not covet. Giving a truthful answer (which I always do) can sometimes add misery to the grief they already feel, so I must be very cautious and often very diplomatic with my responses.

In this instance however, I am certain the answer I give is truthful and uplifting. The short answer I give them is, "Of course not. That would make them unhappy. If they could be unhappy and pining over you in Heaven, how would that be better or different from Earth? But if you are asking me if they remember you, of course they do." It is a response that usually hits the mark.

I also offer them a more considered response. I explain to them that time does not exist in Heaven; that there is no concept of hours or days. Heaven is an eternal day with no night. In Second Peter, the Bible says that one day is as a thousand years and a thousand years as one day.

In other words, there is no concept of time. I explain that if it takes forty more years of living before they can join their pet, it will seem like a very long time to them, but not so for their pet. For their beloved pet, that same forty years will have been like a moment on the eternal clock. When the reunion takes place, it won't feel like forty years had passed. It will be as if they had just seen their human companion moments ago.

I do not mean to make time sound like a bad thing. Of course it is not. It is an absolutely critical element to life on this plane or planet. Every nation, every culture has lived and toiled in the confines of time. Even in places where civilization still mimics the dark ages or where the sun does not shine for months, time is essential to life and living.

Time is a tool given to us by God to keep order in this world. It has served us well. Regardless, it will be refreshing to live without the encumbrances associated with it.

THE PRESENCE AND GLORY OF GOD

Psalms 19:1 tells us "The heavens declare the glory of God . . ."

There are scores of Psalms and other Bible passages that speak to the glory of God. No detail or aspect of Heaven will be more captivating to the human soul than witnessing in person the glory of God. His majestic presence will mesmerize and bless all who behold Him. The never before seen beauty of Heaven, the overwhelming realization of one's earthly faith becoming heavenly sight, the reunions with friends and family—human and animal— will be thoroughly and wholly eclipsed by the presence and glorious countenance of God.

His regal and magnificent presence will illuminate all of Heaven. The light of His glorious person will emanate from seemingly every direction. Not a shadow will be found in our heavenly home. The "Father of lights, with whom is no variableness, neither shadow of turning" (James 1:17) will preclude the need for the former sources of light, Earth's sun and moon.

These two, the sun and moon, have for all of Earth's duration, been our primary source of light and cosmic attention. Their illuminations allowed King David to gaze heavenward in order to pen the words of the Psalm referred to above. Indeed, billions have stared at the heavens contemplating the glory that belongs to God alone. Men have even stood on the moon that David could only gaze upward to see. But the need for it and the sun will be no more.

They shall yield to the greater and superior light and glory of the one who created them. God's glorious presence will be the centerpiece of Heaven for all to worship and adore.

In summary, Heaven is a place of beauty and wonder. I have attempted to paint a glorious picture of this wonderful place, but know my words and thoughts fall far short in describing what awaits those of faith. If I have stimulated your interest and provoked you to think more about eternity, it is enough.

Chapter 6

WHEN WILL HEAVEN BEGIN?

As we have seen in previous chapters, Heaven is not the boring place we might imagine it to be. It is a place of excitement and breathtaking beauty. The majestic and regal presence of God and unfathomable wonder will thrill us for all eternity. There, we will join together in harmony with billions of other humans, angels, and animals to praise and adore our wonderful, loving God. We will understand all that was not clear to us on Earth.

On Earth, our understanding is incomplete. Certain things God reveals to us are not perfectly clear. They cannot be, for our minds are finite and limited. But in this place we know as Heaven, we will be given understanding and we will know. In I Corinthians 13:11-12 we are told

> When I was a child, I spoke as a child, I understood as a child, I thought as a child: but when I became a man, I put away childish things. For now we see through a glass, darkly; but then face to

face: now I know in part; but then shall I know
even as also I am known.

The analogy the Apostle Paul makes is one of being an earthly child. He readily admits that he does not—and therefore we do not—understand all that God has revealed to us in the Bible. In 1 Corinthians 13:12 he states, ". . . now we see through a glass, darkly . . . but then I shall know."

The *then* that he uses twice in this passage is not so much a place as it is a time. To be precise, it is an exact moment—the moment we pass from this earthly life to the next. At that time, in that moment . . . then we will know.

He likens our spiritual shortcomings to that of a child growing up. A child does childish things and understands in a childish way. Children think childish or immature thoughts. But when they become men or women, they put away childish things. Similarly, in our present condition as finite creatures, when it comes to understanding higher, infinite things, we are spiritually immature children. We know only in part the things of God. That day when our hope shall become reality, we will be made spiritually mature. We will understand and know.

When will that day come? When will Heaven become a reality? I actually provided the answer to that question in the wording of the first paragraph of this chapter. Heaven is not *going to be*, Heaven *is*. Right now, today, at this time, Heaven is a reality.

At this very moment, people, angels, and animals are enjoying the bliss of that wonderful place we are discussing. People you have sat and talked with, someone you may have hugged or kissed, loved ones you may have shared intimate moments with, animals you may have pet and played with, are enjoying the beauty and wonder of this place, right now.

My mother and many friends are there, awake and alert, enjoying the splendor we so often talked about while they were still with me. My mother no longer suffers from the dreadful effects of Alzheimer's. Her personality has been restored and she enjoys again the wonderful faculties she possessed on Earth, and then some.

Again, Heaven is not some pie in the sky future dream; it is now. In fact, and forgive me if this comes across as irreverent, Heaven was up and running and open for business long before you and I ever broke into this world.

I know it is difficult to comprehend that Heaven is as real as our present world. We are physical beings whose perceptions trust only what we can see and touch. But remember, in this world we only know *in part*. We only comprehend *in part*. That difficulty of comprehending is a product of our incompleteness, not unbelief. We at least comprehend enough to know that Heaven is real right now.

I live in the United States of America, but people are alive and living in China at this very moment. I have never seen them. I have never been there. But I am confident they are real. There is evidence. I have Chinese friends who have been there and told me about it. I have seen news clips from Beijing. I have seen footage of the Olympics recently held there. I only know of China *in part*, but it is enough for me to know it exists.

So, too, we have evidences about Heaven. We have the Bible. We have the account of the rich man and Lazarus. We have the personal testimony of Jesus. Evidence shows there are people living there right now. I have not seen them (except for those I knew on Earth). I have not been there. But I am confident this place is real, and that it is real now.

Having said all that, I understand people want an answer with more substance. They want to know when Heaven will happen for them. Of course, I cannot know or predict when that might occur on an individual basis, but generally speaking, I think I can clear up any misunderstandings and misconceptions.

Some have been taught there is an intermediate place some must go to in order to appease God, before they can secure a place in Heaven. If you embrace such a belief, it may surprise you to know there is absolutely no support in scripture for this idea. Not one of the thirty-five or so writers God breathed His Word through ever alluded to such a place or concept in any of the accepted Biblical canon of sixty-six books.

Some erroneously claim I Peter 3:18-19 teaches this doctrine, that Jesus gave lost or troubled spirits the opportunity to repent. Let us look at this passage of scripture.

*For Christ also has once suffered for sins, the just
for the unjust, that he might bring us to God, being
put to death in the flesh, but quickened by the
Spirit. By which also he went and preached unto
the spirits in prison.*

The first thing I see is that this verse is in concert with all the other scripture that tells us salvation is through Christ and Christ alone. It tells us that Christ suffered for sin. He was the just one, given for the unjust that he (and no one else) might bring us to God.

This tells me that Jesus Christ procured our place in Heaven because he is just, not us. We are unjust and therefore can do nothing to procure our own salvation. To presumptuously ignore that and say that someone could go to this intermediate place of penance to earn their salvation themselves is an affront to the life, death, and resurrection of the Just One, Jesus the Christ.

Well then, why was he preaching to the spirits there? Doesn't the fact that he was preaching indicate they were being given another chance to repent?

At face value, it may seem that way, but that is not at all what this passage says. Faithful translation of the passage shows that the word *preaching* is translated to mean *heralding* or proclaiming important news. Who or what was he heralding? He was obviously heralding himself.

Jesus is declared in scripture to be the Lord of Lords and King of Kings. We are told in Romans 14:11 that "Every knee shall bow and every tongue confess that Jesus Christ is Lord." Jesus was fulfilling this scripture, ensuring that those knees and tongues knew and confessed (or recognized) who he was. He was showing them that he alone is the King of Glory with power of death. He alone had risen from the dead. He alone had the power to exit the grave and come to that place and leave again.

It is no more complicated than that. When one tries to insert the doctrine of intermediate penance into the verse, it becomes complicated, so much so that it is irreconcilable with other scripture on the doctrine of sin and salvation.

One rule of exegesis every reader of the Bible should know is this—the Word of God never puts itself in conflict with itself. If it appears to you that it has, then you have erred in your interpretation and understanding and you need to start over. If your interpretation is ninety-five percent right, it is wrong. If it is ninety-nine percent right, it is still wrong. The word of God is right one hundred percent of the time and never comes up short.

It appears the origin of this erroneous teaching of an intermediate place of penance stems from the teachings of pagan and secular philosophers, years before this passage in scripture was ever available. It seems there needed to be a way for someone who was sure to suffer under the wrath of God to have a way to make things right with Him.

Meeting that challenge, men like the Greek philosopher Plato and the Roman poet Virgil, championed that need. They hatched and developed the idea of an intermediate state of being where one could pay penance for a sinful life.

As in most philosophical undertakings, they had no Biblical basis for their conclusions, but rather relied upon their own "deep" thoughts and feelings as justification. There is much more to the story. If you are interested in finding out more, there are several good books available on the subject. I would recommend that any study include Alexander Hislop's splendidly documented book, *The Two Babylons*.

For the record, the following scripture tells us the time for reconciliation is in this life and those who pass from this life will either be numbered among the redeemed or numbered among the unjust or lost dead based upon the decision they make on Earth, concerning Jesus. The time to do business with God is now. There is no opportunity or second chance afforded after death.

Isaiah 38:18 tells us

> *For the grave cannot praise thee, death cannot cele-*
> *brate thee: they that go down into the pit cannot*
> *hope for thy truth.*

There is no shortage of ideas about this so-called intermediate place of penance, all of which are erroneous. Variations serve only to further confuse an already confusing topic, which causes people to be unsure of what constitutes salvation, what doctrines they can trust in spiritual matters, and the eschatological chain of events associated with the afterlife.

God is not the author of confusion. Confusion comes from false doctrine, which is the offspring of false ideas. We will try to address these potential confusing topics and fit them in at the appropriate time as we proceed along. But for now, let's concentrate on the question of when Heaven begins.

Obviously, the answer to the question is that the usual way (I almost said most popular way, but thought better of it) people leave this life and move on to the next is through death. I say *usual*, because heretofore the mortality rate has not been one hundred percent. Twice in the history of mankind, Godly men have gone on to Heaven without having gone through the process of death.

The first was a man named Enoch. Genesis 5:24 does not go into great detail about the event. We are simply told that on this occasion "Enoch walked with God and he was not, for God took him." We cannot be sure why or how God effected this *taking*, but we know that Enoch pleased God and that God decided he was not going to die the way men normally do. And so he took him.

We do, however, know a little about the man. Enoch was the father of Methuselah, the man accredited with having lived longer than any other man in history. Methuselah lived to the ripe old age of 969. We also know that the words *walked with God* form phraseology akin to the term we use for Christian service and deportment, today. The "Christian walk" speaks to continual faithfulness and obedience. So we know Enoch was a faithful man.

Enoch lived another three hundred years after Methuselah was born. During that time, his deportment and faithfulness were such that they pleased God. God enjoyed the fellowship He shared with Enoch and wanted it to continue.

Imagine what it was like for this man to be walking with God and for God to say, "Enoch, instead of going home today, how about you come home with me." Okay, that is a dramatization, but I am pretty sure something like that actually happened, because Enoch walked with God and he was not, for God took him.

The next fellow who did not taste of death was the prophet Elijah. He was used in amazing ways by God, so much so that he is perhaps the best known of the many prophets we are told about in the Old Testament.

Perhaps his most celebrated activities were his battle with Ahab, the evil King of Israel and his wicked wife Jezebel; his having been fed providentially by ravens in the wilderness; his battle with the four hundred false prophets of Baal on Mt. Carmel; and the way he passed from this Earth.

His exit from Earth was not quite as simple as Enoch's. In fact, it was nothing short of miraculous. With his student Elisha looking on, Elijah was swept off the Earth by a chariot of fire (II Kings 2:11). The fiery horses and chariot swooped down from the heavens, picked him up, rode a whirlwind back up, and Elijah was no more. Wow! I thought the ultimate cool is being picked up in a limo, but Elijah has that beat hands down.

These two men did not experience death. A lot of speculation revolves around why this is and what God's plan is. One theory is that they will be the two witnesses who come down from God and are slain by the Antichrist during the Great Tribulation. It is theorized that had they died and received their glorified bodies (those that cannot die), they could not come back and be slain as these two witnesses will be.

Some theologians speculate Enoch and Elijah probably did actually die and we are not interpreting the passage correctly. I find this theory lacking and a very problematic fit with the wording and intent of the passage.

It always amazes me how difficult taking what God says at face value is for some people. Why do intellectuals always imagine there is some secret code or message in Bible passages? God writes simply so the common, simple person, like me, can understand what He says. What would be the sense of giving us the Bible if everything was in code and you needed the special Rooty Toot Theological Seminary Special Code Ring to decipher what was said?

The Bible says these men did not die and I prefer to believe it. Whatever the reason, both instances of these men not experiencing death were for specific, providential causes that do not concern us here in this study. Suffice it to say, I subscribe to the theory that they will be the two witnesses. Of all the theories out there, this one makes more sense to me. But again, it is not important to this study.

But before I let it go completely, I have to say that I am a bit jealous of these two men. Who would not prefer their fate to death? Unfortunately, since those times, the lot of mankind has been that we all pass away through death. The Bible confirms this in Hebrews 9:27.

And as it is appointed unto men once to die . . .

I have never purposely misrepresented anything in the Word of God. I made a few transliteration errors while teaching when I was inexperienced and unskilled in the Bible many years ago, but never have I intentionally misrepresented it. If ever there was a verse I was tempted to misquote, it would be this one.

Of course, I jest. I would never alter the meaning of something the Bible teaches. It is just hard to accept that Hebrews 9:27 tells us emphatically that we are all going to die. No matter what, death is in the future for every one of us. How I wish that were not so and that I did not have to tell others it was so. But alas, it is.

God says it is "appointed" unto us once to die. Just what does that mean? Does it mean, as some suppose, that God has picked out a day for us to die, that he arbitrarily selects days and ways for us to die? No, it does not. Of course it does not. Admittedly, there are times when God requires the life of people as written in 1 John 5:16 as "sin unto death," but generally speaking, this is not the case.

God does not choose the day—or the way, for that matter—

we are going to die. As the omniscient (all knowing) God, He looks into the future and knows when it will happen. So then, that time is the appointed time. It is appointed, not by God, but by time and fate.

It is a humbling thought to know that God knows exactly when I am going to die, that he knows how I am going to die, where I will be when I die, and how I will react to dying. But the idea that he directs or appoints it is not supported by scripture.

Indeed, the only way he associates himself with the death of believers is to tell us "Precious in the sight of the Lord is the death of his saints." (Psalms 116:15). Our passing, whenever and however it occurs, is dear to the Lord. He is touched by our suffering and passing. He loves us.

In fact, this love God has for us is the focus of a very peculiar scene revealed to us in John 11:35. We are given a glimpse of the love-generated grief God feels for our passing. I think it would be uplifting for me to share it with you. We are given two simple, but extremely potent words. "Jesus wept."

This is perhaps the oddest passage of scripture you will find in the New Testament. There may be other passages that confuse you or that you do not fully understand, but this certainly could be the oddest. It gives us a picture of God, in the person of the Son, Jesus Christ, weeping.

We are purposely exposed to the tears of God. Before I became familiar with the Bible, I would have never dreamt that God weeps. I mean, this is a shocking revelation. God doesn't cry. Why would he? He is in charge. If He doesn't like something, if something grieves Him, He can change it with a snap of His fingers. And yet, the facts are not in dispute. He wept.

This verse confused me. It bothered me, because it made no sense. Jesus wept, but had no apparent reason to weep. Though he was in man's flesh, he was very God. God doesn't weep, does He?

Even a mind governed by faith that accepts God at His word on everything cannot pass by this text without having a few questions. Why was Jesus so upset? Why did he weep? What does it take to make God cry? For those answers, we must back up a few moments before verse thirty-five to see things from Jesus' eyes, to feel what he was feeling. We must view those moments from God's perspective rather than our own.

In the preceding verses of John Chapter 11, we are told of Jesus receiving word of the passing of Lazarus, a very dear and close disciple. We are also told of the lack of faith of the disciples with him when he received that news and how they determined to go and die with Lazarus (because he was a well-beloved friend to them as well) rather than acknowledge that Jesus could raise him. You may read John Chapter 11 at your leisure, of course, but I think it is an accurate representation.

When Jesus arrived in Bethany and was approaching the home of Lazarus and his sisters, he saw many weeping Jews in the house, including Mary, who previously had gone out to meet the Lord at his arrival. When he observed the scene of grief and weeping, we are told in John 11:33 that he " . . . groaned in the spirit and was troubled." He and Mary exchanged a few words and it is then we are told that the Lord wept.

Some have erroneously supposed that Jesus wept because, like so many others before him, he really was nothing more than a self-proclaimed, powerless prophet. Others claim that maybe he was a true prophet, but when faced with a challenge that required divine intervention, he was not able to enlist God's help and was reduced to tears of frustration.

Those in these camps of thought qualify their fraudulent charges by supposing that when Lazarus was raised, it was not a raising at all, but rather an awakening. Although there is no historical evidence or record to support their view, they suppose that Lazarus suffered from a medical condition that made him appear to be dead and that he awoke at just the right time to make Jesus look good.

The evidence shows that all in attendance were sure that Lazarus had died. We must defer to their eyewitness testimony. They were there. We were not. The average person in those times was probably more exposed to death than any of us are today. I am sure there was no doubt in their minds that Lazarus had passed away.

They had already performed burial rights and prepared his body, something they could hardly do had warmth or breath remained. His own sister had witnessed his body beginning to deteriorate, when she surmised in John 11:39 "Lord by this time he stinketh." So the argument that Lazarus was not actually dead is baseless and unsupportable.

Still, Jesus wept, and I think it is important that we understand why. This was a very profound event. Later, at Gethsemane, he would weep once again, but would drop tears of blood, something a bit more understandable for the God who was to voluntarily die for the sins of the world at the will of the Father. In that situation, he said, ". . . .not my will Father, but thine . . ." (Luke 22:42).

But the situation was not the same at Bethany. Jesus had complete control. He knew he was going to raise Lazarus in just a few moments. Earlier, on the road to Bethany, he had acknowledged this when he told the disciples in verse eleven "I go that I may awake him out of sleep." There simply was no reason for heaviness of heart. Or was there?

Too often, when we hold God on the high pedestal He so richly deserves, we somehow forget that one of His characteristics is love. A critical component of true love is the presence of a compassionate heart. Jesus, as the God-man, was the epitome of compassion. It is no stretch to think that all that was going on caused him deep, personal grief.

Consider that he had just spent several days traveling with disciples who had largely expressed a lack of faith and whose mood was, at best, somber. Surely seeing this lack of faith in them did not please him.

Then, as he moved into the burial area, he was overwhelmed by the prevailing air of grief. As he moved among the people he loved, he saw their sorrow, he saw their defeat, their weeping and wailing fell upon his ears, and he was deeply troubled by it.

The only breath of encouragement that found its way to the Lord was that of Martha, one of the sisters of Lazarus. As he came near to the city, she came out to meet him and greeted him with her well-known, persevering faith. But even her faith was framed in grief and sorrow.

Again, Jesus knew he was about to raise Lazarus. He knew

that in a few moments there would be great joy and the sorrow of the moment would be gone and forgotten. He knew he would turn their tears to smiles and their heartache to praise. Soon all would be well . . . for them.

But for Jesus, there was more than just the heartache of the moment. As he surveyed the scene of mourning due to the passing of Lazarus, he was thinking about the cause rather than the effect of death. Jesus was looking beyond the obvious, beyond the weeping crowd and mourners, and lamenting how much suffering sin had brought to his creation.

For just a brief moment, he thought on man's history. He remembered the very moment when Adam chose to sin and how his disobedience had broken God's heart. He remembered how the seed of sin was passed on from Adam to his son. He remembered when Cain rose up in jealousy and anger against his brother and how Abel's blood cried out to Him from the ground.

He recalled the destruction of Sodom and Gomorrah and how Abraham could not find even ten righteous people in the whole of the cities so God could spare them. Jesus thought of all the evil and wickedness that had taken root among those God had created in his own image, of the ravages of sin on His perfect creation, and he groaned in his spirit and was troubled (John 11:33).

As he thought back on man's infamous history, he also looked forward to the cross and the price he would have to pay for sin even though he had never sinned himself. Surrounded by the unbelief of his closest followers and immersed in this scene of sorrow, no doubt the burden was great as he considered all these things and moved among the mourners.

He saw their pain, he felt their sorrow, and their weeping stirred his heart. The sting of death, brought upon man because of sin, was doing its evil work. He saw the pain, he saw the misery, he saw the wages of sin being paid out and the heart of God was broken for the people He had created. And my friend, *Jesus wept!*

His heart was broken for God's creation. Our sin brought Almighty God to tears. In retrospect, I suppose this verse is really not that odd after all. It perfectly expresses the love God has for each and every one of us.

I apologize for the short detour, but I felt it was important to frame death in the proper context. The only way to get to Heaven, short of the rapture (which we will discuss next) is through death. The result of all life on Earth is death. There is no other way.

You may leave this world in a spaceship, but not this life. You may build a fortress that forbids the entry of any and all enemies, but death will find you. Some may live large, others small, but all funnel through the same conduit of death to exit this life. There are no exceptions, other than the two special individuals we previously identified.

You may exercise every day, take vitamin supplements, have a check-up annually, and eat the healthiest food. You may not smoke, drink alcohol, or take illicit drugs. You may have received artificial organs or medical enhancements to prolong your life. It simply does not matter. The mortality rate for us on Earth is still one hundred percent. You and I are going to die. That is currently the only way of leaving this life and getting to Heaven.

But there is another way coming; a one-time event that will preclude the need of death. I am sure you know. It is called the rapture. The word *rapture* does not appear in the Bible. Rather, it is an endearing term Christians have adopted to express what the Bible calls the "snatching away" of the Church.

Briefly, when the Lord returns to Earth in the clouds, he will command believers to "Come up hither" (Revelation 11:12) because He will have us meet Him in the air as He will not set foot on the Earth. At that time, not only will living believers be supernaturally lifted from the Earth and changed to the incorruptible vessel we spoke of earlier, but those believers who have previously passed away will rise and have their bodies restored and changed as well. The souls of those resurrected will have been housed in temporary tabernacles (bodies) in Heaven pending this great day. Together, with living believers, they comprise the Church or the Bride of Christ and all will be whisked away to Heaven while the Great Tribulation takes place on Earth.

The rapture could happen at any moment. There is no eschatological checklist that needs to be completed before the Lord's return. Those prophecies associated with the rapture are all things that will occur *after* the snatching away of the Bride of Christ, the church. Nothing is preventing the Lord from returning for us at any moment. That ought to be a sobering thought.

This promise, this snatching away, is exclusively for believers, those who have accepted God's terms for reconciliation through His Son, the Lord Jesus. I know many have imagined a set of scales in God's hands, where He measures their good and bad, but that is not Biblical. And quite frankly, it is a very convenient cop out.

If you were to stop one hundred people on the street and ask them if they were going to Heaven, most, if not all would answer the question by responding, "Yes, I am a good person." They would assess themselves as worthy. Curiously, almost without exception, everyone who weighs their own good and bad tip the scales in their own favor. Go figure!

We may not feel as if we are stellar people in God's eyes, but certainly we are no worse than the next guy or girl. We buy into that age-old devil's lie that God somehow measures our worth by what good we may have done.

Well, the truth is that God does not have a set of scales and he does not judge us based upon good or bad. He has already assessed us humans collectively and individually and the news is not good. He says of the good we have done that it ". . . is as filthy rags"(Isaiah 64:6) and that we have no righteousness in and of ourselves. In Romans 3:19 he assesses the entire human race and caps it off by saying we are all guilty before Him.

Pretty harsh words I know, but He does not exact them in a condemning way. Rather, he simply is telling us that we need Him and He pleads with us to trust His Son, who is the only way to reconcile with Him. Jesus said, "I am the way, the truth and the life; no man cometh unto the Father but by me" (John 14:6).

I do not want to be too preachy here, but if you have never accepted him, you may want to consider doing so. The rapture is an exclusive event. All are invited, but to be a part of it, you must RVSP the invitation in the way God prescribes.

We cannot discuss the rapture without addressing the inevitable question *When will the rapture occur?* As I said above, the rapture can occur at any time. There is nothing preventing it from happening right now, prophetically speaking. But there are some obvious indicators to watch for.

All the "signs" the Lord spoke of signal the rise of the Antichrist and his coming to power during the Great Tribulation. Many of those signs are now being seen, from devastating inflation and economies failing to governmental corruption on a scale never before seen, to name a few. Since the snatching away of the Church occurs before the advent of Antichrist, and since that seems to be nearer than ever, it follows that the rapture is imminent.

We are indeed seeing strong evidence of the world preparing for a one-world leader like Antichrist. The Lord warned this day would come as a thief in the night, without warning. But He added a disclaimer to that warning for believers. He told us that it would not be as a thief to believers; that we would see that day approaching.

As a Christian, as a Biblicist and theologian who pays attention to current events, I see that day approaching. I have written about it at length in other forums. I have even identified who I think the Antichrist will be; that is how close I believe it is. Some will scoff, but I assure you that the case I build is solid and unimpeachable. It is not some baseless, New-Age rubbish.

I am not flippant and always exercise great caution when I try to interpret and apply scripture in light of current events. I am well aware of the many in history who have laid claim to special or extra revelation from God about some great event that they claim is to occur. A good example is William Miller, a Baptist, who, for lack of a better term, went off the deep end. Miller claimed that he had special revelation (which should be the first warning signal to anyone listening) that the Lord Jesus would return on March 21, 1844.

Of course, despite all the hoopla he created and his detailed preparation for departure on that day, nothing happened. He was shamed, and well he should have been. No one, absolutely no one can receive special or additional revelation from God. The Bible says in Matthew 24:36, "But of that day and hour knoweth no man, no not the angels or heaven, but my Father only." But the story doesn't end there for poor Mr. Miller. After doing some nifty re-calculations, he determined that he had made a mathematical error. In fact, the rapture was not to occur for another seven months. The new date was set for October 22, 1844. This time the result was going to be different, he promised.

Well, the only thing different was that he did not prepare alone. Many of his followers joined him. His followers sold their possessions. Some sold their homes. Others sold their businesses. Many packed travel bags (for what reason I am not sure, because we can take nothing with us) and joined him to wait on a hill for this blessed event to occur. But of course, again, it didn't.

After this total public humiliation, Miller retired from public view, at least for a while. While secluded, Miller released this statement:

> *I waited all Tuesday (October 22) and dear*
> *Jesus did not come; I waited all the forenoon of*
> *Wednesday, and was well in body as I ever was,*

but after 12 o'clock I began to feel faint, and before
dark I needed someone to help me up to my
chamber, as my natural strength was leaving me
very fast, and I lay prostrate for 2 days without
any pain, sick with disappointment.

There is so much I could say about this character, but I will be gracious and let the account of his folly speak for itself. I appreciate that I could use his self-inflicted miserable experiences for some good.

My point is that I am well aware of the peril of making predictions or adding things to the Bible that are not there. My conclusion that the rapture is nearer than ever before is not a result of some extra revelation from God. I would never claim that, and the day I do, may the Lord pull a mountain over on top of me and take me home.

It is rather, an educated and considered conclusion drawn from regimented, reverential study of the Word of God, with an eye on world events. Without doubt, the end is nearing. It is almost upon us. I say that, not as one of those fanatical, misguided doomsday sign bearers, but as someone who knows the Bible and sees that day approaching.

I know the difference between fanaticism and trying to educate others to the dangers coming. I recall as a teenager, sitting in a restaurant in Honolulu with my parents. Across and down the street was a large, illuminated sign on a church that said simply, THE END IS COMING.

I will not identify the church by name, but I am sure that

anyone who lived on the island of Oahu in the last half of the twentieth century will know the one I speak of. It was as much a landmark as the cross at Camp Smith, the Dole Pineapple-shaped water tower, Chinaman's Hat, or any other well-known local places of renown.

I am ashamed to say that when I first saw that sign in 1966, I chuckled to myself while shaking my head in disdain at what I perceived to be the closed-minded fanaticism of religious people. Since being wholly and thoroughly converted to Christianity and finding myself agreeing with that message, but I am wise enough to know that to announce that Biblical teaching in such a judgmental fashion still evokes the same dismissive response.

I do not mean to offend anyone. I want to provoke readers to think more seriously about the implications of what the Bible says the future holds. After all, this book is about a heavenly reunion. It makes sense then to discuss the most important aspects of what it takes to ensure that reunion—death, rapture, and salvation. Certain prophecies have a bearing on our understanding of these things, so it is prudent to highlight them and discuss them.

Contrary to secular misconception, the end time event is not something that will happen overnight while we sleep, like the erroneous claims of Y2K or the Mayan doomsday event of 2012. It actually will entail a very long process. For example, should that process begin today, it will take 1,007 years to complete as two distinct periods known as the Great Tribulation and Final Millennium must first occur. Since they have obviously not yet occurred, they remain on the prophetic calendar. They do not precede the rapture, but they do occur prior to the end of time.

Another misconception is that the phrase "the end is coming" means that mankind is about to be extinguished. Not so; the Bible does not teach this. Humanity will never be extinguished or cease to exist. The Bible teaches quite the opposite; collectively and individually, life is eternal for all of us. Where you spend that eternity is another question, but we will not address that here.

Nevertheless, there is an expiration date for this old earth and life as we know it here. I have heard many of my contemporary ministers radically and emphatically declare that the end is truly near, meaning that the 1,007 year period is about to commence, not that human life will be extinguished. "The signs" they assert, "are everywhere."

Their warning is usually presented with an urgency that mirrors someone yelling, "Fire!" or "Shark!" They stir people up or they upset them, all in an attempt to manipulate or sway them to their way of thinking. I am all for winning someone to the Bible point of view—doing so is in their best interest—but I do not believe we can be so pragmatic about doing the job that we cast off ethical conduct.

While I agree with their end game assessment about this world ending, up until this point I have refrained from what I term the "chicken-little" approach to eschatology or end time things. I have, heretofore, restrained myself from trying to interpret the signs and times. Too many well-intentioned believers have made fools of themselves—like our friend William Miller—in years past trying to anticipate or second-guess the Lord.

In the past, I did not see that times or signs were lining up quite in the way the scripture warned us they would. I justified my thinking with recollections of far worse times on Earth than we have today. For instance, the Bubonic Plague, Spanish Inquisition, or the Holocaust. Surely during these times, through unfathomable suffering and heartache, people of faith must have thought the world was at its evil apogee and that God would come. But He did not.

There was good reason for this. It was not yet the time. Certain things had to come to pass or be in place globally before that corrupt one would be accepted and welcomed by a world in chaos. I discuss them in my dissertation on the Antichrist in my book *Difficult Things of the Bible Explained,* so I will not discuss them in detail here.

But I would like to discuss one factor. I hold it to be a key issue to this prophetic event of the Antichrist rising to power in the end times. I see it coming to pass now. It is no longer a future event.

This factor is rampant corruption at all governmental levels. Corruption is defined as the purposeful change from good to evil in morals and actions. I am the first to admit that everyone has a measure of corruptness or immorality in them. You do, I do. We all do. It is part of our human nature. Most of us wish it were not so, but it is, and that is just the way things are.

Let me give you an example of what I am saying. I recall a discussion in my favorite psychology class years ago. The class, largely liberal politically and ideologically, was asked to discuss the morality of a fictional man's action. His wife was dying of cancer. The local pharmacist had in stock the medicine that would cure his wife, but it was very expensive. In fact, the medicine cost thousands of dollars above what the unfortunate man was able to pay.

He pleaded with the pharmacist, promising to pay over time, but he was denied the medicine. He tried finding sponsors or contributors, but was unsuccessful. In desperation, the man broke into the pharmacy during the night and stole the medicine that his wife needed and ultimately the medicine did its job and she was spared.

The class was asked if the action the man took was moral and right. Almost without exception (me being the sole dissenter) the class decided the man in the hypothetical story was both right and moral to take the action he took. Though I was openly mocked by the professor and the class for my unpopular position that the man acted wrongfully, I did not lose my cool as I tried to explain my position.

I pointed out to the class that I was not saying that I would not have done exactly what the man had done. I was certain that given the same circumstances I would have broken the law, violated the civil rights of the pharmacist, and robbed him of his merchandise. I probably would have done exactly what the man had done. The difference was that I would have known and admitted openly that what I did was wrong and immoral.

The class either could not or would not concede that breaking and entering, and stealing was wrong in this situation. It was in other situations, but the seriousness of one's needs pragmatically outweighed the morals and ethics of law and society. This is an excellent example of corruptness at work—when the morality of an individual or group goes purposely from good to bad because internally they legitimize it to themselves.

It is this attitude, this corruption and immorality, that will signal the rise of the Antichrist and ultimately "the end" that follows. I am not speaking of the corruption of individuals (for we have always had that), but corruption at the governmental level on a global scale. I think we can all agree that the government of the United States is not only the most important player in global politics but the standard bearer; as the United States goes, so goes other world governments. Our government will play a pivotal role in hastening the coming end.

The growing corruptness of local and federal governments in this country is disturbing. Surely you have been aghast at the shenanigans of our own bicameral Congress—from special provisions allowing insider trading when it is a capital offense for ordinary citizens, to evasion of taxes without any thought of penalization. It seems our politicians have designed laws to allow them to break them with impunity.

It is more than personal gain that motivates them toward corruption. Sometimes the motivation is a bit more noble; for instance, to help the community coffers. Let me just grab a few of the stories that made current headlines when I began work on this chapter. On the local level, one county in California arbitrarily decided to ban Frisbee and ball throwing on beaches, under the threat of a hundred-dollar fine. The reason given is they wanted to safeguard the safety of other beachgoers who might be injured during these activities.

Okay, I can accept that safety could be an issue, except that for a nominal fee, you can get a permit that then allows you to throw Frisbees or balls on that same beach. Somehow, by paying the permit fee and carrying an authorization in your pocket, the activities are magically safer. The safety of others is not at risk.

On the federal level, the administration recently mandated that religious organizations violate their religious beliefs and provide birth control for their employees. I was thrilled to see that it evoked a strong and concerted reaction from religious organizations across denominational lines, but the fact remains, the government is corrupt, purposely attacking the Constitutional rights of "We the people" in order to achieve their ulterior agenda. I would say that qualifies as departing from doing good in order to do evil.

The more corrupt government becomes, the more governmental power grows (from a relinquishing of personal rights). Corruption is a raging fire in government and the flames are being fanned by progressive ideologues. Government, the Bible (Romans 13:4) says should be ". . . a minister of good," but it is far from being that. It seems government now epitomizes the old cliché "Power corrupts, absolute power corrupts absolutely." There can be no denying that governments world-wide are absolutely corrupt.

It is corruption that will usher in the "Corrupt One." Once again, throughout my Christian experience, though often tempted by current events, I have been reluctant to publish that I thought the Lord's return was imminent. It seemed to me that our harsh times were no worse and probably much better than the harshness of other times, so it seemed to me that my expectation of the Lord coming during my lifetime should not be high.

But my opinion has changed. It has changed because the critical factors of Biblically-defined end times are now starting to rapidly fall into place. Absolute corruptness is the key to ushering in the one who is known as corruption personified and his time is almost here. But before he gets here, before that final 1,007 years begins, Jesus Christ will come to snatch his believers away in the rapture.

In summary, Heaven is a place that is happening right now. It is not some future event, but has proactively been growing as believers pass from this world to it every day. If you can wrap your mind around that and embrace it, the truth of it will grow exponentially within you until it becomes a source of great comfort and hope.

Chapter 7

OUR REUNION WITH GOD

A glorious day is coming. It will be unlike any day ever experienced here on Earth or for that matter, in Heaven. There is going to be a grand reunion in Heaven. That is not the only good news. What makes this day even greater is that it will be a never ending day. On Earth, days we looked forward to with great anticipation came and passed so quickly they were over and behind us before we even realized it. Not so this day of reunion in that heavenly land. This day will go on without end. The experience will be continuous as we will remain in the presence of God and all who worship Him eternally.

There have been a handful of days of equal, perhaps even greater, importance on Earth. Those days marked the birth, death, resurrection, and ascension of Jesus Christ, the Son of God. As monumental as each of those days were, they all pointed forward to this grand day of reunion. In fact, their purpose was to ensure this grand day—the reunion of mankind with God—would one day be realized.

Our reunion with God will be just the beginning. That blessed event will be followed by mini-reunions with friends, family, and our wonderful animal friends. Undoubtedly, the most important reunion will be with our creator, God. To be ushered into the presence of the Lord, to see the one who paid the price for our admission there, will overshadow any other earthly or eternal experience.

That should not diminish the importance and excitement of seeing our loved ones. Those reunions will be grand times, as well. It will be difficult for me to explain the mechanics and timeline because, as we have seen previously, there is no time or timeline in Heaven, but I will give it my best effort.

Time as we know it does not exist in Heaven. It is imperative to understand that. Our existence on Earth is measureable. It is temporal. Our life in Heaven cannot be measured. It is going to be eternal. We will not segment events or compartmentalize and ration our time as we did here on Earth. However, as I unfold for you how I envision the reunion taking place, I will necessarily define the experience in terms of time, as it is the only conceptual tool available to me in my finite condition.

The heavenly experience will be so different from what we have known in our four dimensional world on Earth. You may try to rationalize it, but your efforts will fail as have mine and a thousand theologians before me. We do not have the capacity in our current state to fully understand the complexity and wonder of Heaven.

Let me present you with one of the more complex and deeper elements of the next life you may not have considered. Take just a moment to think about what I say and try to answer for yourself the question I pose, and you should come to the realization

that there just is no possible answer. No doubt we will understand when the Lord gives us understanding, but for now it is
just not to be.

I am sure that we can agree that Heaven, or whatever you are
inclined to call the next life, is an eternal place. We shall live forever and never die again, life without end. Isn't that what eternal means? Without end? Well actually, that is only part of the
definition of this word. There is more to it than that, but most
people never consider the whole meaning.

The Bible tells us that Jesus is eternal. That means his life is
without end. But when the Bible explains Jesus' existence, it says
that it is more than just life without end. We are told that he has
no beginning or end of days, that he is the same yesterday, today,
and forever. He is truly eternal. He not only will exist forever,
but he has always existed. He has no end, but he has no beginning either.

The same wording used to address the eternalness of Jesus is
used when describing our eternity. When we reconcile with God,
he gives us eternal life. It is the same word with the same meaning. If it is eternal, the rendering is not only that we will live forever, but that we have always been alive.

Wow, that is a new slant on an old understanding, is it not?
But the definition has always been the same. It only seems like
a new slant, because you are hearing it for the first time. But
still, one must ask, how is that possible? How can it be?

I envision intellectuals and fellow theologians raising their
eyebrows on that one. I can see them attributing what I just said
to my having fallen away from the truth or otherwise compro-

mising my Biblicist stand. Some may even accuse me of giving myself over to some sort of Zen enlightenment or other eastern philosophy.

But that is nonsense. Rest assured that I am a strict Biblicist. I am not trying to cause a stir or to grab my fifteen minutes of fame with some revolutionary, heretical doctrine as so many religious television personalities attempt to do. I am simply saying that words mean things and the definition of this word *eternal* cannot be denied. The word cannot be made to mean other than it means. Eternal means no beginning and no end.

When the Lord uses it in a certain way in one instance, we have a reasonable expectation that when he uses it somewhere else in the Bible, it retains the same meaning. That meaning is that there is no beginning and no end. My eternal life was guaranteed when I accepted the Lord. But if it is truly eternal, it has always existed; it didn't start on the day I accepted him.

Okay, you are thinking, *I get the idea, but explain to me how that can be.* I can't. I don't know. Nobody knows . . . at least nobody here on Earth. That is my point. Heaven is a very complex reality to understand from the current plane we exist on. I am sure that there is no shortage of pseudo-theologians who will try to explain it, but invariably their explanations will fail. It is just one of those things we are not able to know in this life no matter how earnest we are in trying to discover it.

Take, for instance, the Godhead. I have read a dozen explanations on how God can be one God and yet three persons, ranging from comparison to an egg (shell, white, and yoke) to likening the Godhead to water (ice, liquid, and steam). I have yet to have one of these illustrations give me understanding. I still do not understand how God can be one God, but three separate personages. But I know it is so.

How is it that I cannot see God the Father, but I can see God the Son? I get that the Father is spirit and the Son is the express image of the Godhead, but how does that work? My finite existence allows me to grasp the concept, but not to understand the details. One day I shall, but it is not for me to know now, only to accept by faith.

The semantics of what the word *eternal* means does not really matter to me. My understanding or lack of understanding does not change anything in my relationship with God. Similarly, understanding the Godhead will not increase or decrease my faith or change my standing with God. What matters most to me, especially from the standpoint of a person who loves his animals, what I really want to know, is what the reunion or reunions will be like in Heaven.

We have already identified that there will be more than one reunion and I will discuss them in great detail. So there is no confusion, these reunions will be based on entering Heaven by someone who has passed away. It will not represent what happens after the rapture.

Reunions via the rapture will not occur in quite the same way. For one thing, the sheer number of believers entering the kingdom will dictate that the grand reunion will not be as personal or individualized as when someone passes from this world to the next. Additionally, when the rapture occurs, there are several events that will take place in Heaven that may delay other reunion events.

One such event is the Judgment Seat of Christ or the Bema Seat judgment where Christ judges the faithful service (not sin) of his followers and rewards them with any of five different crowns that can be earned. Then there is also the Marriage Supper of the Lamb. You have undoubtedly heard, and probably yourself used the term *A marriage made in Heaven*. Sadly, while few earthly or human marriages last very long these days, the good news is that the marriage of the Bride of Christ (the church) to the Bridegroom (Jesus) will be a perfect and lasting union.

There will be an actual ceremony and it will be a very regal event. While there will undoubtedly be wonderful mini-reunions going on all over the great banquet hall, the focus will be on our union with Christ and not our reunion with any other person or animal.

For those reasons, I think it is prudent to discuss the reunions of the individual arriving in Heaven through death rather than the masses at the rapture. But do not be concerned that our reunion with God and those we love will be diminished in any way at the rapture. It will just happen differently.

As believers pass from this life, they will close their eyes to this world and instantaneously open them in the next. The Lord said that believers ". . . shall not come into condemnation, but are passed from death unto life" (John 5:24). There is no soul sleep, no total annihilation of the soul or spirit, and no intermediate place of penance. Those false teachings are the concoctions of people who were anxious about the type of life they had lived and who felt they were in danger of stirring the anger and wrath of God. They needed a safety net, so they created one.

Believers, when they pass, are whisked away supernaturally

to that heavenly shore. It is commonly accepted, from several places in scripture, that we are escorted to our heavenly home by angels. These angels appear not to be our guardians or rather guarding angels, but special messengers sent from God.

It is true that our body remains behind, but the body is just the shell. Our flesh is not who we are. We are not bodies with souls, but rather souls with bodies. To some that may sound as if it is just a play on words with no significant difference, but it is not. We are not our body. We are our soul.

The soul is the seat of our consciousness. It is where our cognitive process occurs, where our personality resides, where emotions are housed. The body is merely the machine that allows us movement and the sensation we call senses. It is the soul that controls.

Death of the body is the absence of the soul. Our soul departs the body the moment the body expires and immediately we are present with the Lord. No matter how philosophically Eastern that may sound, it is sound Bible teaching.

Again, we will have an immediate grand reunion with God, followed by many mini-reunions with friends, families, and pets. While all of these reunions are important, none are more important than our reunion with God, of course. But I am not forgetting that the focus of this book is the reunion we expect to have with our departed pets. So, while I will touch on all the reunions, I will concentrate more on painting a comprehensive picture of what our reunion with our pets will be like.

Determining my approach to this chapter was a difficult process for me. Initially, I thought of taking the cowardly way of just elaborating upon the Bible passages that tell us about

Heaven. But I felt that this would come across as sterile and surgical and undoubtedly bore readers. So I dismissed this idea rather quickly.

Next, I toyed with the idea of simply sharing with readers what it was that motivated me to want to write on this topic, including a series of graphic and detailed dreams about Heaven that seemed as if God was communicating with me. But that did not seem like a great idea, either.

When you tell others you had a dream and God spoke to you in that dream, the usual conclusion they come to is that you are at best overly zealous and at worst, a kook. No one wants to be called a kook.

I knew a man, a friend I suppose, who had become somewhat of a religious fanatic. He meant well, but went off the deep end and, well, got all weird. On a flight from Hawaii to California, years before 9-11 and the safety sanctions that are now imposed on all flights, he got out of his seat and walked into the cockpit to talk to the pilot.

In those days, you could do things like that without too much of a stir. Instead of being startled, the pilot said, "Yes sir, what can I do for you?"

My friend said, "God just spoke to me and told me to tell you to turn this plane around. He said someone was waiting for me back at the Honolulu airport."

Apparently the pilot believed him, because he did in fact, turn the plane around.

It turned out my friend was right, too. Someone was actually waiting for him at the airport—the FBI! He was arrested and charged.

This story is true and I have not embellished the facts at all. You just can't make things like this up.

Because of things like that, I am reluctant to say that God spoke to me in a dream. When such a claim is made, some imagine that God gave the person a special revelation. But any seasoned Christian knows that God condemns such claims (for example, in Revelation 22:18–19). Most believers know that God does not speak to people today as he once did to Moses, David, Paul and others, and for good reason. His revelation (the Bible) is complete. We have all that He wanted us to have. There is no more to come.

But God does speak to us in our hearts and minds. We are told specifically that the Holy Spirit, who dwells in each believer, speaks to our hearts and burdens us with impressions or thoughts on issues such as mission or deportment.

This type of communication from God is neither claimed to be, nor should it be misconstrued to be, a special or extra revelation from God. Nothing of this sort is canonical or inspired. It is merely God speaking to the heart of His child to exact some behavior or growth from within that is always in concert with something He already has said in the Bible.

Dreams once were a method by which God spoke to His servants and those of faith. This is not some oddball, New Age idea. There are many examples of people experiencing God-directed dreams throughout scripture. God revealed truths through dreams that He caused believers and unbelievers to have to effect His will and purpose—people like King Nebuchadnezzar, King of Babylon in the book of Daniel.

God advertised that he would use dreams to speak to people. In Joel 2:28–29 we are told:

> *And it shall come to pass afterward, that I will pour out my spirit upon all flesh; and your sons and your daughters shall prophesy, your old men shall dream dreams, your young men shall see visions; and also upon the servants and upon the handmaids in those days will I pour out my spirit.*

I am not trying to pull a spiritual sleight of hand on you here. I know that this passage is speaking of the last days and special circumstances. I would not try to cause you to believe otherwise. But this revelation, coupled with the examples we have with how God used dreams to speak through and to people, establishes the fact that God does use dreams.

Again, I will be the first one to affirm that God will never reveal more truth than is already revealed in His Word. The Bible is the complete and holy revelation of Jesus Christ to the world. God will never, never, never violate His own edict that nothing should be added to or taken away from this record.

But nothing prevents God from speaking to His children in their hearts and minds for personal growth and edification. I am certain that at times, and admittedly infrequently, God visits me in the night season to speak to my heart. Often it is just to convict me of a sin or shortcoming in my life, but sometimes it is to direct or influence my way of thinking so I become a better Christian or help others in their time of need, spiritual or otherwise.

In I Kings, Chapter 19 we are given the story of the Prophet Elijah hiding in a cave on Mt. Horeb. He was one of two men who did not taste death. He went to Heaven in a chariot of fire, a fitting flamboyant end for a man who lived life large for the Lord.

I'm sorry if that sounds irreverent to either Elijah or the Lord. It is not meant to. I just do not know how else to say it in modern vernacular in order to capture the essence of the great way God used him. His was a life of extraordinarily large faith and power.

In the same chapter of 1 Kings we find this great man of God hiding in a cave in fear. Just previous to this, he had been on Mt. Carmel doing spiritual battle with four hundred prophets of the false god Baal. They mocked him and his God, and threatened him. But God overthrew those cultists through Elijah in a mighty way and the people rose up and slew all four hundred false prophets.

Ahab, the evil king of Israel, who himself was a Baal worshipper, lamented the defeat of the false prophets to his wife, the infamous Jezebel. Jezebel, in anger, took an oath to slay Elijah. For reasons that remain a mystery to me, this great man Elijah, who had successfully destroyed all the false prophets, and quite possibly undermined the cults' hold on the people of Israel, panicked. He took flight and found a cave in Horeb to hide and fret in.

But God was not about to let him hide in fear or be distressed. He decided to speak to Elijah. And the method by which he chose to speak to him, I think God still employs today when he speaks to His children. Let's read I Kings 19:11–12 to see how God spoke to the heart of Elijah.

And behold, the Lord passed by, and a great and
strong wind rent the mountains, and brake in
pieces the rocks before the Lord; but the Lord was
not in the wind: and after the wind an earthquake;
but the Lord was not in the earthquake: and after
the earthquake a fire; but the Lord was not in the
fire: and after the fire a still small voice.

It was this still, small voice that spoke to Elijah and brought him out of the cave so God could use him again. The equivalent for the Christian is found in John 10:27 where Jesus said, "My sheep hear my voice. . . ." The children of God know when God speaks to them, and God often speaks to us in our dreams and quiet times.

God has spoken to me many times via my dreams and quiet times. He often stirs me to better service or convicts me of sin. He burdens my heart for someone in need. Occasionally, I am rousted out of my sleep and impressed to pray for someone in the wee hours of the morning. He also uses my dreams to give me understanding of difficult scriptures I have struggled with.

In light of all that, it is not outrageous for me to believe He speaks to me in my dreams or thoughts about Heaven. When we study a topic earnestly and prayerfully seek God's guidance in understanding something, is it not reasonable to expect that He will answer in the affirmative and help us to understand? Of course it is. If it were not, then why would He tell us to pray? Indeed, why would we bother to pray?

That said, we, and therefore I, must be careful in discerning some of the things with which God's still, small voice impresses us. As I have written about in detail in the past, sometimes the things God puts on my heart, the way he deals with me from within, are for private consumption only.

In *Wagging Tails in Heaven* I labeled this aspect of God speaking to His child as "Private Comforting." Often, when His children are suffering emotional trauma, God the loving Father will speak to their hearts in a way that only they can understand and appreciate. No one else could benefit from it, only the one spoken to.

I used one of my own experiences as an example of this, in the aforementioned book, *Wagging Tails in Heaven*. I won't revisit it here in detail except to say that God spoke to me in a way that only I could understand. He impressed me with thoughts that could only come from Him, thoughts about things I had long forgotten, but He hadn't.

The effect was that when I was at my lowest point, the experience served to convince me that my dog Samantha was alive and well. If you are inclined to either acquaint or remind yourself about this experience, you will find it on page 226 of that book.

There I purposely point out that this experience was for me and no one else, though others were able to benefit from knowing about it. That is why I must be careful in discernment. Sharing word for word from my private dreams does not seem like the right thing to do at times. It is too difficult for me to know what is meant exclusively for me, to help me, and what is meant to give me insight to help others.

It seems more prudent to use a combination of scripture, personal knowledge, experiences, and things I know to be from God—impressions, perceptions, and of course, dreams—to build a hypothetical picture of what our reunions will be like.

Additionally, to animate that picture and add meat to what is said, I am actually going to use myself as an example. I am going to visualize my own passing and arrival in Heaven and let you follow along.

Some might question why I feel that I am qualified to write on this topic of a reunion with our pets at all, and that would be a legitimate question. I do not only feel that I am qualified, but I believe that I am most qualified. I do not mean that in a proud or boastful way, quite the contrary.

I am humbled to find myself ministering to those who are suffering and brokenhearted. I would never have guessed that I would be used in this way. But when God allowed my own heart to be broken, He was preparing me to assimilate to and with others who would experience traumatic pet losses of their own.

It wasn't by mistake that He laid Isaiah 61:1 on my heart. It has been the springboard for my ministry and the fuel for my passion to help others.

The Spirit of the Lord God is upon me; because the Lord hath anointed me to preach good tidings unto the meek; he hath sent me to bind up the broken hearted, to proclaim liberty to the captives, and the opening of the prison to them that are bound.

He was also placing a burden upon me to research and become expert at all He has to say about His animals and His providential and eternal care for them. Accordingly, I have spent more time in the last twenty years researching the topic of animal souls and animal afterlife than any of my fellows.

If you were able to look back at my footsteps in this undertaking, you would find that prior to the release of my first book, *Cold Noses at the Pearly Gates* in 1996, there was effectively nothing of significance written on this subject. I searched the Library of Congress, the Internet, the brick and mortar libraries of several major cities, and many religious encyclopedias, and uncovered nothing substantial.

There were brief mentions of the importance of animals to God by authors such as C. S. Lewis and others of his time, but no mention of animals having souls or an afterlife. Many a preacher and Christian author made mention of animals in their writings, but the ideas were fleeting and nothing of substance.

The famed twelfth-century Italian Catholic, Francis of Assisi, did much on behalf of animals. He often championed their welfare in local venues, wrote about their worth to God and man, developed prayers to be used for their benefit, and laid the groundwork for today's modern animal blessing services that many Catholics and people of other denominations observe.

He did not address the more weighty matters of animals' eternal essences and God's providence. He was not overly concerned with those matters. His interest was in their proper care in the here and now. There are records of his having preached to birds, but the content of his thoughts to them seem to have been of no consequence in terms of spiritual things; not that it would have mattered as animals have no spiritual awareness in this life, a topic that I cover in detail in other titles.

In fact, the truth be known, he was not the constantly wandering animal minister many painted him to be. He did his share of traveling, but his time was spent founding religious orders for men and women and helping them to flourish and grow. I do not mean to diminish all that he did on behalf of animals. He certainly deserves credit for being the humanitarian that he was, but his writings about them were not theologically reaching or mature.

Despite an exhaustive search, I found that nothing significant had ever been written that addressed the eternity of animals. As a consequence, to know what the Bible said about animals, I had to do the research myself. Accordingly, I spent several months identifying and researching every passage that even briefly mentioned animals in the Bible.

Immediately, it proved to be more difficult than I had expected. I discovered that the word *animal* does not appear in scripture. As I mentioned earlier, the Bible uses words and phrases like *beasts, creatures, every living thing,* and *all that have breath* to name but a few. Before I could search out the verses that addressed animals, I had to perform significant research to discover the various ways animals were referred to.

I performed word search analysis, cross referencing every phrase and word in the Greek and Hebrew, whichever applied to a particular passage; regularly consulted several major commentaries; and also read many of the writings of Jewish historians. I believe I nearly wore out my copy of *Strong's Exhaustive Concordance* in my research.

I kept extensive notes and reviewed and rechecked them regularly. In time, I categorized the information I had accumulated and was able to draw solid conclusions, which I now teach. It is important to note that my research initially was conducted for nothing more than self edification. It was only after I had developed and organized the material into a comprehensive outline that the idea of publishing the findings to benefit others occurred.

Since first publishing my work in 1996, several hundred of my fellow ministers have taken exception with my work, though I found later that they had never researched the topic themselves. Most had just scanned my books and had no idea what they were about, but had somehow concluded that I was wrong. All but a very few (perhaps a half dozen) were willing to discuss the matter and give me an opportunity to make the case they had not taken the time to read about in my books.

All but one of the hundreds of objectors I spoke with changed their position after being presented the evidence. Numbered among those who were honest enough to admit their error was the chancellor of a major Christian college, a well-known television evangelist, and scores of fellow ministers and pastors.

I appreciate when men and women will put aside their preconceptions, honestly evaluate the evidence, and yield to the truth of God's Word. I have been on the receiving side of correction in another Bible matter and it is a very humbling experience, but one that made me a better servant.

My point to having said all this is that I believe my qualifications come from being the pioneer in this field of study. Certainly there are many other books on this topic available now, but those books were not available in 1996. They came much later. In fact, many of them were written by people who first read my books and were moved to write their own. I don't mind that at all as long as their motive is to help others.

Few, if any, have sufficient theological backgrounds or credentials to tackle such topics, and their work reflects that as many of the claims made are not Biblical. They have not invested the tens of thousands of hours of study and research required to write authoritatively on the subject matter.

It is my more than sixty thousand hours of professional and personal study of the Bible, coupled with earnest prayer and meditation that qualify me to discuss the reunion in Heaven that awaits people, and in particular pet people, since that is the theme of this book and the genre I pioneered.

Please do not think I am being boastful. I truly am not. I have nothing to boast about. I am merely trying to satisfy the apprehensions of those who would question my qualifications to write on this topic. I am being mechanical in my response as I would be if I were a pilot who was asked why he thought he was qualified to fly, after the plane was in the air.

Since I have opened the proverbial can of worms about theological credentials, please allow me to point out that I feel awkward using the term *theologian* when describing myself or others. In this modern age, the title "Theologian" is often used interchangeably with the title "Bible Scholar."

Both confer some sort of officially recognized pedigree or authority on the one so labeled, a sort of religious seal of approval if you will. This might be acceptable in some circles, but it should not be so. There are too many so-called pedigreed theologians who are nothing more than apostates and heretics.

When I was attending a secular college to pick up a few needed credit hours, I made the mistake of taking an Old Testament Survey course. I was intrigued to know that such curriculum was taught in a non-Christian university. I thought it might be interesting to see what was being taught. I really did not need the course as for many years I had taught such a course myself. I suppose that played into my decision to take it. I thought it would be a breeze and an easy way to pick up three credit hours.

Imagine my surprise to find that it was not a breeze. The professor, falsely called a Bible Scholar and Theologian (oh yes, he held both titles) was an ardent atheist. He was also antagonistic toward those who did believe. He actually cussed God out in class, shaking his fist wildly in the air at Him and calling Him filthy names to get a rise out of students of faith.

He attempted to belittle God in front of the students. He mocked Him at every possible juncture. He tried to show the class that the Bible was nothing more than historical writings, not equal, and probably not as important as the sacred writings of all other religions. Yet he proudly wore the titles of Bible Scholar and Theologian.

I am so wound up just thinking about that awful man and experience that I am tempted to take a huge rabbit trail here to address his ills and deceits and those of the countless humanistic professors like him. But I will restrain myself from doing so and move along. Suffice it to say that there are many deceivers in this world who cheapen the titles of Bible Scholar and Theologian, and he definitely is at the head of that class.

Degrees and titles do not impress me much and I doubt they impress God at all. I may be formally educated in Bible and Ministry and attended several accredited colleges and universities, but more important than all of that is my personal relationship with God. If my relationship with God is wrong or if I embrace heretical doctrine, what good are my credentials?

Once our relationship with God is right, our academic achievements will be governed by a Godly circumspection and humanism will find no room to pollute our thoughts. Critical to being a trustworthy Biblicist and theologian is to recognize that God comes before knowledge. The Bible says, "The fear of the Lord is the beginning of knowledge . . ." (Proverbs 1:7).

This college professor did not understand that, and I doubt he would have cared if he had. Consequently, his knowledge of the Bible was as fouled as the sum of his life, in terms of knowing and serving God. He was full of himself, but void of God. Yet he held the accepted credentials. Imagine that.

Stepping off my soapbox now, let me move ahead. When I guess or speculate about how our reunion will occur, I do so with complete reverence for God and His Word. My thoughts may seem a little different from your personal ideas about what Heaven will be like, but I assure you that I do not have the cart before the horse as some do.

The single most important element of my qualifications for addressing on this topic is that I love the Word of God. It is God's love letter to me. Oh yes, it is for everyone else, too, but I have to personalize it so that it means what it does to me.

During the Vietnam era, I was deployed overseas on an attack aircraft carrier. For those sailors among you who may wonder which one, I was stationed aboard the USS *Forrestal* (CVA-59). It was a grand old ship with a lot of good sailors onboard, but we had a worthless navigator. He seemed to never be able to find our way home.

Long deployments took a toll on all to be sure, but it seems they were most difficult on young homesick sailors who were in love. The older "salts" were used to being away from home. Indeed, some of them looked forward to it. But it was very hard on the young guys. (I am not being sexist. Women were not assigned to ships in those days.)

At mail call, if at all possible, all work and activities on the ship came to a halt. The noise and clamor of five thousand sailors and airmen and the engines of one hundred aircraft all but fell silent as groups of men gathered about the ship waiting to hear their name called by their respective mail clerks.

Those were the days of no computers or cell phones. How jealous we old salts (sailors) are of today's mariners. They can call home on cell phones, e-mail as often as they like, and even see their family live on their computer screens.

In my day, snail mail was the primary method of communicating with loved ones. You could sign up for a five minute conversation via ham radio if you were so inclined, but the list was long. It usually took several months before your turn came up and then you spent the entire conversation listening mostly to static and squelch noises.

During the actual, long-awaited conversation, the ham operator would usually have to interpret what your wife or girlfriend had said, because the static was so bad. It was embarrassing to have another sailor tell you, "Your wife said she loves you with all her heart" or "She said she bought a new black lace negligee just for you."

If that was not bad enough, there were the constant "dead times" when your wife would forget to say, "over" so the switch could be thrown to allow the other party to talk. It was quite frustrating.

So snail mail at mail call was it, and it was crucial to ship's morale. It was an event that happened only once or twice a week, and since it really was not very disruptive to ship or air operations, shipboard work usually yielded to mail activities. Even when it was not convenient, morale issues usually trumped operations and the skipper made allowances for it.

How I remember the many times I waited to hear my name called. Even if it was just a renewal notice for a magazine, receiving mail stirred thoughts of home and had a dramatic positive impact on my attitude for the rest of the day. But on the days when I received a letter from my wife . . . well, unless you have experienced the pressures of a long deployment in foreign waters, away from the people you love, you cannot understand the thrill.

I recall one particularly long period the ship's crew had to endure without mail service. Operations precluded us from being near a friendly port to retrieve letters and packages. After nearly three weeks, the mail plane finally showed on radar and word spread throughout the ship. A concerted, "yahoo" was heard echoing throughout the passageways and hangar bays.

I received only one letter that day, but it was an eight page beauty. I was very busy when the mail came, involved in air operations, so little time was available. But I found enough time to show up for mail call. The mail clerk held my letter high after calling my name. I rushed up and snatched it out of his hand and found a quiet corner to tear the envelope open.

I only had a few seconds before I was needed in the air traffic control center, so I scanned the several pages looking for the key words every sailor looks for. There they were. *I miss you, I love you, I know you have a job to do. Don't worry, one day you will be home with me.* Whew, I needed that boost in my morale. For at least a while, the pressure was off.

Beaming, I stuffed the letter back into the envelope, stuffed the envelope into my back pocket, and scurried off to work. A few hours later I had a short break. I was supposed to go to chow, but gave that up so I could read my letter. I quickly took it out and began reading it slowly, absorbing every line.

It soothed me. It calmed my fears, the fears that sailors always battle, the insecurities and unknowns. The letter assured me that I was the only one my wife cared about and loved. She had written all the things I needed to hear.

Again I had to stuff the letter away because it was time to get back to work. We had a dozen jets in the air and they were depending upon us to bring them safely back to the ship. But on the next break I read my letter again. It still said the same thing. And then again and again I reread her love letter to me. It gave me great peace and comfort.

The Bible is like that love letter for me. For many, the Bible is a historical record. For others, it is a reference book. But for a Biblicist, it is a love letter from God. When I read it, it isn't just a conglomeration of facts or wisdom. There is a personal message in it for me. As I searched the pages and lines, I find the words I need to hear. The Lord says, "I miss you, I love you, you have a job to do, but don't worry, one day you will be home with me."

The Christian should view God's Word as a love letter. They

ought to be excited by it. They ought to be eager to find time to open it and read it over and over again. Christians need to know what God's love letter says. There can be no guessing. Our commission, and therefore our commitment, is to represent what He says with conviction and certainty. This then, is the qualification that matters to me most, that I know the Word and words of God, the Bible.

Long ago theologians were known as "illuminators." Though they did not have the handy, portable Bibles we have today, they had access to and studied the huge manuscripts and logs available to them. These were men devoted to the study of God's Word and rightly dividing (understanding and interpreting) the word of truth. They would rather be halted in life than misrepresent or misinterpret the Word of God.

They prayerfully and carefully read and reread scripture for marathon sessions until scripture passages were committed to memory. While others were enjoying their leisure at whatever the hobbies of those days were, the illuminators would deny themselves those pleasures and remain immersed in quiet, earnest study of the Bible. While others were furthering their careers or education, these would forfeit their eyesight under inferior candlelight, digesting the truths of God's Word far into the night, every night.

It was said that these men were so familiar with scripture that someone could push a pin through the manuscript they used and the illuminator could tell them what word the pin pierced twenty or thirty pages deep. How many Christians could do that if someone shoved a pin through their Bible?

The Bible is the most important thing on Earth. Anyone and

everyone who speaks of God or spiritual things ought to know this book better than any other thing. That is the goal I have aspired to. That is the only qualification that matters.

I have subordinated my thoughts to what the Bible teaches and I have never and will never purposely misrepresent what God has said. You will find no violation or unrighteous dividing of the word of truth in my writings. Where I speculate, it will be clear that it is my speculation and you can assign it the appropriate weight. I will be the first to admit that my speculation is nothing more than opinion and opinions can be wrong.

But I have spent many, many thousands of hours contemplating the things of God as they pertain to Heaven and what our reunion(s) will be like. I am sure much of what I write will prove to be right, but I have not deluded myself. I know that the half of what God has in store for us cannot be told. I also know that I am operating from a four dimensional understanding and perception, which limits my ability to conceive of most of the wonder of Heaven. I hope you will take that into account as you read on.

So then, without further delay, let's proceed on to a snapshot of what our heavenly reunion with God will be like. Since the premise of our adventure into Heaven will be my own demise, I elect to pass away quietly in my sleep. After all, I want my presentation to be as real as possible and passing in my sleep is truly the way I would prefer to pass.

And so we begin . . .

As I sat up in bed, I was conscious of having been violently shaken, as if someone had just tried desperately to wake me from sleep. I looked around, but could not see anyone. For that matter, I couldn't see anything at all. It seemed to be extraordinarily dark in the house; so dark that I felt that I had lost my sight. Questions started to flood my mind. What had just happened? What jolted me out of my sleep? Why is it so eerily dark in my bedroom? Was there an earthquake? Was the power knocked out? A dozen more questions raced through my mind. It was quite unsettling.

Suddenly, there was a light in the corner of my bedroom. It startled me because I knew there was no light in that part of my bedroom. Then I realized it was not a light at all. It was more like a window on the wall with light flooding in from the outside. Had the power come back on? Was this some sort of a reflection from a light outside?

It wasn't a reflection and it wasn't coming from the outside. It was something else, but I had no idea what it could be. As I studied it, the light or whatever it was slowly grew larger until I could see that it was not on my wall at all. In fact, there was no wall. It seemed to hang on nothing in the blackness.

I thought that I should be wary, but oddly, I felt no apprehension. A sweet peace came over me, and I knew that what was happening was good, very good. I knew that I was in no danger, but still had no idea what was happening. Somehow I knew that I was not asleep and dreaming.

As I watched the light, it continued to grow in size and intensity. But then I realized that I was not getting closer to it, but it was getting closer to me. Within just a few moments, it was upon me, bursting into the darkness, and I was absorbed into it. Immediately, everything was illuminated. The light was intense, but soft and

gentle. It seemed to be alive as it sought out and erased every trace
of darkness.

As my surroundings became visible, I could see that I was not
in my bed. In fact, I was not in my bedroom and I was not sitting. I had been standing through this whole experience, as short
as it had been.

And I immediately noticed something else. I was not alone. On
either side of me was a man helping to steady me. I hadn't realized until that moment that I needed steadying, but my knees did
feel a little wobbly. I had not been aware of the presence of these
men either, but it wasn't a shock. In fact, I felt a sense of gratitude that they were helping me. I made a mental note of how kind
it was of them.

As I focused and took a closer look at the gentlemen, I could
see that they were not men, but angels! Puzzled for just a moment,
I don't know how I knew that, but I did. My mind was racing,
trying to make sense of what was happening, and I realized there
were two possibilities with regards to my situation—either I was
dreaming or I had passed away. I looked searchingly into the face
of the angel on my right side, but before I could speak to ask, he
gently nodded his head to confirm the latter.

"Wow," I thought, "I am dead. I really am dead." That realization did nothing to diminish the peace that had cradled me ever
since this experience began. If anything, the news was comforting.
At least all that I was experiencing made sense now. Though I had
died . . . I didn't feel dead . . . I mean I was awake and alert. I was
making conscious observations and feeling emotions of joy and peace.
Death was proving to not be so bad after all.

It seemed that my awareness was growing, not just as a result *of having been thrust from darkness into light, but something inside me seemed to be awakening. A I possessed an awareness I had never known before. I also felt a peace unlike any peace I had experienced before.*

Employing this new heightened awareness, I took a better look at the two beings at my side. They had a different countenance than men, a subordinate, yet regal air about them, as servants of a king would possess.

Surprisingly, I could see no wings. I was sure that angels had wings. It was one of the things I remembered about them in my study of scripture. Before I could ponder that question at length, my mind understood that their wings were kept out of sight on different occasions, such as when they were in human form. Instead of wondering why they had no wings, I found myself wondering how they managed to keep them out of sight when they wanted to.

I quickly left off wondering about their wings and thought about the changes that were coming over me. Though the changes were subtle, they were not unnoticeable. My awareness and understanding were growing, and it dawned on me that the change Christians will undergo is not immediate, but a process that must be realized step by step as one is assimilated into this new life. I could feel the process taking place. Each moment seemed to bring a new understanding or perception, and I wondered how long it would take.

I could not keep myself from wondering about these two angels. I was not surprised by their presence, especially knowing that my earthly life had ended, but I could not help feeling that I had seen one of them on Earth.

I found myself uttering my first words in eternity. "Haven't I seen you before sir?" I asked the angel nearest me.

He confirmed that I had by answering, "Yes, you saw me on several occasions. I was put in human form to be a help at a church you used to attend. We never spoke, but we did sit next to each other on several occasions."

I found myself surprised that I was not surprised by his response and simply responded, "Oh, I thought so." Then I added "Were you my guardian angel?"

He smiled gently. "You mean guarding angel. I am not a guarding angel. You had two who helped you on Earth, but they also had others they watched over and they remain at their duties. I am a messenger."

I recalled from my Bible studies that a messenger is a general description of angels, or at least their assigned responsibilities. The Greek word for angel means exactly that: messenger. The role of a messenger is to simply bring the message or will of God to man. Almost exclusively, this was a method employed by God in the days before scripture was compiled and readily available to mankind.

My assumption that they were my guardian or guarding angels spoken about in Matthew 18:10 and Hebrews 1:14 was understandable. They seemed to be helping me and I made the reasonable assumption that they were guarding me in my new life. It did not take me long to figure out that there was no need for guarding in Heaven. It is a place of constant peace under the watchful eye of the Almighty.

As I absorbed his response, I noticed that we were moving. It was different from flying as I understood flying back on Earth. We seemed to move forward by some unseen force. There was nothing to see around us at the moment, so I am not sure how I had the sensation of movement. We just were, well, transporting.

It seemed clear to me that entering the illuminated place was my passing from death unto life. Leaving the darkness of death behind and arriving so quickly was the fulfillment of what the Lord had told us that passing from death unto life would be.

I slowly awakened to the wonder of this new life and was suddenly conscious of changes in my body that I hadn't noticed earlier. I felt strong and healthy. The pain from the separated shoulder and bone spur that I had lived with for so many years was gone. My other aches and pains also were no more.

I felt youthful again. There were no graying hairs, wrinkles, blemishes, or any of the fleshy ills of Earth. And the amazing thing was, I knew these things to be true without even looking in a mirror.

With every new awareness and realization, I became increasingly more excited. I likened the feeling to waking from a ten year coma, slowly regaining motor skills, and learning about all the changes that have taken place in the world. As I made the comparison, I basked in my growing sense of joy over the new perceptive abilities I was experiencing. I suppose in a way, I was awakening too.

My visual perception was the next of my senses to grow. Before me, as if it had just materialized into view, was a panoramic cosmic view of several stars and planets. They did not appear to be very far away. In fact, they seemed to be extraordinarily close. The planet closest seemed to be much larger than Earth's moon when it is at its closest point to Earth. Perhaps it was twenty times larger than an earthly full moon. It nearly filled the sky. It certainly dominated my attention at the moment.

There was a definite 3-D effect, too. I felt I could just reach out and touch the planet, but of course, I couldn't. The picturesque view was everywhere; to our sides, in front of us, behind us, above us, and even below us. In fact, far beneath my feet was a planet that looked like Earth. It was Earth! It boggled my mind.

Turning to one of the angels, I asked for an explanation and was told that the planets were real and that they were there, but that we were not actually there, at least not in a physical sense. We were on another plane of existence. We could see Earth, for instance, but people on Earth could not see us.

That answer satisfied me as I was becoming accustomed to the impossible. In any event, I understood that I didn't have to understand for something to be the way it was. It was the way it was, regardless of whether I understood it or not.

We moved again and were in the midst of vast fields of color, surrounded by strikingly decorated hills and trees unlike any I had ever seen before. The cosmic view was suddenly gone. Oddly, I had not seen it disappear or move, but it was gone. In its place was a sky of different hues of blue that seemed more beautiful than was possible. Like everything else I had seen, it was a breathtaking sight.

Great cities began to unfold around us. One moment they were not there and the next we were in the midst of them. Each city had its own glow or hue, with an effervescence of colors rising above it. Once again, I marveled at what I was seeing. And again, it simply was unlike anything I had ever seen or heard about before.

Each city was adorned with different precious gems and stones of varying brilliance. Each gem was tremendous, nearly the size of a football. The streets were brilliant and radiant, and yet again, unlike anything I had previously experienced.

As we neared one of the cities, I was impressed with the cleanliness of it. Though my eyes made only a quick, sweeping search, I saw no trash, no fading colors, no unkemptness, not even a stray leaf. I *could not even find a shadow, for the light of this new and wondrous place illuminated every conceivable place where a shadow might lurk.*

There were many, many people. They did not look much different from people back on Earth, except that everyone appeared to be the same height. No one was shorter or taller, at least not noticeably. Without exception, all seemed to be at peace. Contentment seemed to prevail.

I do not mean to convey an image of lethargy or to suggest that the people were dronish in attitude or demeanor. Quite the contrary. There was much excitement in the air and I perceived myriad upbeat, happy personalities interacting with one another. Contentment was the only word I could find to describe what I saw.

It did not seem anything like what I was accustomed to on Earth. People on Earth converse and interact all the time, but often they are loud or abrasive. There was none of that.

The ambiance was different. There was none of the hustle-bustle chaos of Earth. There were no sounds of sirens wailing in the distance, no clamorous noise of industry or construction, no automobiles or trains. Everything was serene. The only sound apart from the pleasant conversations taking place was the sweet, almost hushed sound of a choir.

Suddenly, it was like my senses were on steroids. The peaceful silence was broken by the sound of thousands of sweet voices wafting through the air. But wait, that is not an adequate or appropriate assessment. The silence was complimented, the ear intoxicated with the indescribably pleasant chorus of worshipful voices.

The sound of it caused my mind to recall the many times my lips had sung the words to Charles Wesley's hymn "Oh For a Thousand Tongues to Sing." Undoubtedly, this Godly harmony of voices was what the hymnist had in mind as he penned the uplifting words. A thousand tongues (and much more) were indeed singing the praises of God.

I could not make out any of the words the choir was singing, if indeed there were any. Now, I could not be sure if what I was hearing was music or if it was voices of such harmony they sounded like music. Combined with the pleasant, picturesque landscape, the sound was very soothing . . . and harmonic. My mind raced back to I Corinthians 2:9, ". . . eye hath not seen, nor ear heard . . ." Truly this verse captured my feelings.

Content as I was to sit and listen, my escorted journey continued on. Shortly, my complete attention was refocused upon a glow directly ahead of us. It was like seeing the glow of a great city when you are driving at night as you get nearer to the city. This was similar, but the light was so very much more intense.

In the blink of an eye, it was right before us. It was like the glow of the white flame of a welding torch, but more brilliant and more intense than that. And yet, it was pleasant to my eyes and not uncomfortable at all.

Looking upon that brilliant light, I remembered being a teenager and challenged by a friend to stare at the bright light of the torch a nearby welder was holding. He told me that it would hurt my eyes if I did, but up for any stupid challenge, I assured him I could do it and proceeded to stare. After about thirty seconds I turned to him and said, "See my eyes are fine, you idiot."

The next morning I discovered that I had actually been the idiot. I woke up to find that someone had pulled my eyelids back in my sleep and poured sand into my eyes. Not really; it only felt as if someone had. Nevertheless, I was in excruciating pain.

The doctor told me that the damage was minor and would quickly heal. He also said that it had been a long time since he had treated a fool who stared at a welder's torch. And I thought doctors were to do no harm.

And he wasn't through with me. He capped off the visit by asking me a question. "Wasn't the man wearing a darkened face guard? What do you think he wears it for?" I knew it was a rhetorical question because he left the room shaking his head and didn't wait for my answer.

The glow of this light before me was vastly more intense than a welder's torch, but it did my eyes no harm. It wasn't diminished by the first illumination, either. In fact, just the opposite was true. This new glow, though embedded in the larger area of illumination, stood out more brilliantly than the illumination surrounding it.

Once again, I called upon my Earthly experiences as comparison. When I attended Navy firefighting school I learned how to fight magnesium fires. Magnesium burns brilliantly and is very difficult to extinguish. It cannot be extinguished with water. Actually, it will burn underwater. One of the illustrations at school was to burn a piece of magnesium in the school's indoor swimming pool.

For effect, the pool lights were lit up while the building lights were dimmed. The pool was a dazzling light in the darkness. But when the magnesium was set on fire and thrown into the pool, the light of the pool paled to the brilliance of the burning magnesium.

As I thought of that experience, I realized it was the closest way to describe the dazzling light in the midst of the illumination of Heaven.

It dawned on me that this light was holy light. It was the presence of the person of Almighty God. I was being ushered into His *presence by my escort angels. But before I could adjust to the force and impact of that overwhelming thought, I was before the Lord.*

I don't know exactly how I came to be directly in front of the Almighty. I may have walked under my own power or perhaps the angels escorted me there. I cannot be sure, but the latter seems more likely. I am sure that I wasn't wrestled into His presence kicking and screaming like some hapless peasant before a demanding, evil king, but was gently escorted by the angels in the same manner they had treated me from the first.

Emotion welled up inside of me. The swelling of my essence and life reacted to being in the presence of the giver of life. The feeling was incredible.

I only had a moment to glimpse my surroundings for humility was already forcing me to my knees, but I did manage to take one sweeping look at the heavenly throne room of God. Ordinarily, one would not be expected to recall such a scene in detail with just a fleeting glimpse. But the passages in scripture that describe this scene were so familiar to me and so vividly accurate I had no trouble registering the glorious details of the scene.

Briefly, the four and twenty elders were there, of course. They seemed pleased to see me, but didn't show any special attention to my presence. Some were actively paying homage to the Lord, while others ministered or conversed with each other.

The beautiful sea of glass, which was like crystal, stretched out farther than I had imagined, even unto the distant multitude of believers and angels that knelt in reverence. I noted that the sweet chorus I had been hearing came from this great multitude. They had indeed been singing and their voices were pure and holy.

What an amazing musical concept; that voices could be so pure and blend so perfectly they actually sounded like music. I knew that on Earth the voices of siblings often blended perfectly with each other. I knew that a cappella groups could imitate musical instruments, and some very cleverly. But never on Earth was anything as sweetly pure as the sound I was hearing. If I closed my eyes, I thought I was hearing an orchestra and not the blended voices of praise.

I did not understand how so great a multitude could be present in this great throne room when I had seen so many outside, but I was sure knowledge and understanding would come in time. I did see how the Lord could refer to His many followers as a "cloud" of witnesses, for truly the sheer number in white made the mass appear as clouds.

The rainbow around the throne was exceedingly beautiful. It was not like the rainbows on Earth, but rather complete and not a half. The colors were every color I had ever seen and more. I had always thought the word bow described a bend in something, like an arch. Now, I understood it meant a continuous arching or circle, too.

The beasts with varying appearances and the seven burning lamps were around the throne, but it was the throne itself that demanded my attention. I had expected lightning and thunder and voices proceeding out from it as Revelation, Chapter Four tells us. I realized almost immediately that those would be present during the Seal Judgments and not before.

None of this deterred my attention from the regal majesty of the one who sat on the throne. The sight of Him was magnificent. I felt weak and fell to my knees. I knew how John had felt when he fell before the Lord's feet as a dead man (Revelation 1:17). I felt *so unworthy and yet so special. I was in the presence of the Almighty. He was looking at me. And like John, I fell on my face in adoration before Him.*

Though I felt I wanted to lift my head and speak feelings of adoration and love I could not. My mouth would not form the words and my mind was numb. The only thought that came to me was Revelation 8:1, which says, "And when he had opened the seventh seal, there was silence in Heaven about the space of half an hour."

That verse did not apply to anything but the total awe for God's wrath being poured out during the Great Tribulation, but for some reason the wording was fitting because I was so astonished at the majesty and greatness of God that I could not speak. There He was, right in front of me, my faith turned to sight, and I could do nothing but adore Him. I was truly awestruck.

I beheld the essence of the Father, but of course, I could not see His face. It was not for me to see, even as He had said many times in scripture. Still, His presence was overwhelming, almost too much to take in. I felt pleasant, like the times I had indulged in too much chocolate. His majesty and glory was simply indescribable.

Beside Him, at His right hand, was the one with whom we have to do, the express image of the Godhead, the only begotten of the Father, the Lord Jesus Christ. At last, I was in the presence of the one who so loved me, that he laid his life down willingly for me. At last my faith was sight and I beheld my blessed Lord and Savior. Like his Father, his countenance was brilliant and astonishing.

The reunion was all that the Bible told us it would be. The Lord welcomed me and commended my service. But he also confirmed that at the Bema Seat he would be reviewing my works as a Chris-

tian. *Of course, there would be no mention of sin, as all my sin was under the blood and forgotten by the Father; but what works I did in the new life that God gave me would come under review.*

I won't go into the details of what was said to me. First, some of it was a little too embarrassing. I knew that I had failed the Lord many times in many ways, and he confirmed it, but not in a condemning way. He just seemed disappointed, which probably made me feel worse than a scolding might have.

He made me realize how many friends and coworkers were to miss Heaven because I had, at times, been remiss in my responsibility to bring the gospel message to them. He knew I had not been ashamed of Him or embarrassed to discuss the gospel. I had just grown weary of wrestling with people over their erroneous views. Consequently, I got lazy. But he also lauded the many good things I had done to ease the burden of other saints, the many thousands of souls I had shared the gospel with, and my work for Him.

I guess this proved the change was a step-by-step process. I was able to feel shame and regret at my failings. And I knew that at the Bema Seat I would probably feel even worse. But I knew, too, that this would only be a one-time experience and very short-lived as it gave place to the joy and happiness promised.

We spoke for what seemed to be a very long time, but I am sure it was only a few moments on eternity's scale. The Lord spoke to me on a personal level, more as a friend than anything else. He reminded me of moments in my life that I had long forgotten. He shared with me that he knew my heart when often it seemed others did not.

He knew that I cared about people and that I cared about them for the right reason; because he cared about them. He knew how many thousands of hours I had spent communicating with strangers, helping them with their problems and feelings. That seemed to be a big thing with him. And I felt sort of proud, but in a good way, happy that I had pleased him.

It was amazingly important to me that God knew who I was and what I was made of. We have all suffered at the hands or words of people who misread us. Life on Earth was very frustrating. It seemed there was no hero to sweep in and make things in life right, simply by understanding. How wonderful to know that there is such a hero in Heaven.

I have no idea how it was possible for me to have monopolized so much of the Lord's time, as I was sure other believers were arriving all the time. No doubt they were going to go through the same process and required the Lord's time, as well. But knowing that time does not exist in eternity, I figured it was probably not all that difficult for the Lord to accomplish.

Eventually, our meeting did come to a close, but as much as I did not want it to, there was no sadness. The Lord assured me that we would spend much time together during eternity. For now, he wanted me to spend time with loved ones who were waiting to see me. He knew that was important to me and them.

Heaven was not at all what I had expected. It was so very much more and so very much better. Truly what God had prepared had not entered into my heart on Earth.

Chapter 8

OUR REUNION WITH FRIENDS

I t is difficult to describe the experience of meeting God face-to-face in anything but earthly terms, especially given that my passing was, after all, hypothetical. I have never actually been to Heaven, so my ability to describe what the reunion will be like is limited to my fourth-dimensional understanding or earthly perspective.

I offer insights based upon a combination of details offered in scripture, personal interpretations and impressions, and experiences and dreams. Admittedly, I am sprinkling in a dash of imagination, but confident the paragraphs below give a fairly faithful snapshot of Heaven and not some weird New Age or sci-fi distortion.

In Heaven, during the meeting with God, I came to understand that knowledge and awareness had increased substantially, and would continue to grow with each new experience as it unfolded. Words on the topic were not exchanged. Nevertheless, somehow I knew.

I was reminded that the tabernacle (my body) was a temporary arrangement, although I had not realized I was in a temporary body as my appearance was essentially the same . . . except that I was more youthful and robust. In my life on Earth I had been aware that the Bible taught that pre-rapture Christians who passed away would be given temporary bodies, but in the excitement of entering Heaven I hadn't remembered.

With that reminder came the understanding that eventually, my original body would be resurrected and undergo the change that is promised in I Corinthians, chapter 15. When that occurred, the knowledge of all believers still in temporary tabernacles would be increased exponentially, we would understand all things, and receive our permanent, glorified bodies. Until then, apparently, we had only the enhanced faculties necessary to assimilate into our new life.

When my long awaited initial face-to-face meeting with the Lord was complete, I was escorted again by the two angels who had companioned me earlier, but I was not out of the presence of the Father. His Spirit was in every corner of Heaven and in that sense, He was omnipresent. I could feel his presence with me and with all the others I came into contact with as we moved along.

Travel was nothing like Earth. We did not walk. We could have if we had wanted to I suppose, but we did not. We did not fly, but also probably could have if we had so desired. We just moved to new locations by desiring to be there.

Unlike consciously willing ourselves transported to another location like in some earthly sci-fi movie, it was more a spontaneous occurrence. It was as simple as facing in the direction we wanted to go and the place was just there before us.

While I did not quite understand their connection to my travel, undoubtedly, my two angel companions had something to do with it. They apparently also had keen powers of perception, appearing to know what was on my mind. Suffice it to say that they knew my desires and my questions before I articulated them.

From my studies of scripture, I remembered that angels were not all-knowing so I knew they were not reading my mind. Often, on Earth, people believed that angels had the power to know what we were thinking. For instance, some thought that Satan, who himself is an angel, had the ability to read minds and know the future and that he could use this power against us in some way. But he does not have that ability. Scripture tells us that God alone possesses that sort of power (Matthew 13:32 and 24:36).

Somehow those two angels knew that I wanted to see family and friends. I suppose that it logically made sense that arriving humans would desire to see loved ones first and that was certainly my case. I was eager to meet with those I had known and loved on Earth.

We turned and were immediately in a huge hall, larger than any man-made structure I had experienced on Earth—bigger than any sports stadium and perhaps larger than all of them combined. As far as I could see in every direction, the hall continued on. There was no horizon bow in my line of vision, but eventually, it got hazy, much like a mirage on Earth.

If I made a conscious effort to refocus, everything instantly became clear. Seeing seemingly miles away without much effort was a new experience and dimension I wanted to explore, but I turned my attention to what was happening immediately around me.

The detailed décor of the structure was solid gold, but it was the magnificent floor that impressed me the most. It was not fine marble or transparent gold as other parts of heaven had been described to be. Rather, it appeared to be grass . . . but not like any grass that I had ever seen before.

The general appearance was a mixture of blue, green, and gold, but hues of every color were mixed in—beautiful, glittering colors, some of which I had never seen before. The grass glistened as if it was wet, but when I stooped to touch it, it was not.

But it was not actually dry either. It was slick-smooth like the finest silk, softer than the imitation rabbit fur gloves I had as a child, and sweet to the touch. Somehow the touching of it gave me the mouthwatering sensation of chocolate.

Suddenly, I became aware of people around me—many, many people. I hadn't noticed them before because of my preoccupation with the beauty of the hall and grass, or perhaps they had just arrived. New experiences were happening at a rapid rate, and it was proving difficult to keep up with all the activity.

People were everywhere, strolling on the pathway that led through the grass, sitting on the walls of the fountains I hadn't noticed, either, and milling around. Some were talking in small groups, while others sat or walked alone.

Before I could ask my companions how I would be able to find loved ones, I heard a voice call out softly, "Gary, I am here." My heart thrilled. I knew that voice. It belonged to my mother. I had been thinking about her since my arrival. Well, truth be told, a day had not gone by since her passing that I hadn't thought about her.

From the very first moment of my arrival in Heaven, I had been overwhelmed with emotion and preoccupied with my surroundings, but I had also been searching the faces of those we came across, hoping to see her. I knew I would see her eventually, because she had accepted the Lord many years before and was assured of a place in Heaven. I just wasn't sure when that reunion would take place.

But here she was, my sweet mom, the one who loved me though forced to endure every frightful and harrowing experience that a boy could throw at her. I embraced her and it was like I was a young child again. I felt safe and at ease. It isn't that I felt unsafe or ill at ease; quite the contrary. Heaven was already proving to be the place of perfect peace and harmony that the Lord promised it would be. It was just that in that brief moment I was reminded of the bond a child shares with their mother and I felt added comfort and peace.

It was truly as grand a reunion as I had anticipated. I embraced her, feeling like a child again, safe and at ease. Holding her at arm's length for a moment, I noted that she was youthful again. The gray hairs were gone, and her face was smooth and lovely. Oddly, that was not a surprise. We used to speculate together in our talks about Heaven that we would be youthful again.

For me, that meant mid-thirties. In my thirties, it was the prime of my life. I was healthier, heartier, and more full of energy than at any other time in my many years. If I was given a choice at what age I would like to be, it would be thirty-three, coincidentally, the same age Jesus was when his earthly life ended.

As I took in my mother's image, I realized age probably didn't matter, anyway. She looked youthful and well, as did everyone around us.

I began to recognize their faces—relatives, friends and co-workers. All were smiling, some offered a greeting, and some stopped to give me a quick hug.

It seemed that everyone I knew was there. But how was that possible? I felt sure that several members of my family and many of my co-workers had rejected the Bible saying that God did not exist. They had rejected Him and not been recipients of His grace. How then could they be in Heaven?

I turned to the angels with a questioning look. One explained that I retained only the memories of those who had been born again. Therefore, I could not miss anyone I did not remember and that was why it seemed to me that everyone I knew was there. That meant there were some in my life whom I had forgotten. Strangely, that revelation did not make me sad. Somehow I understood and accepted it. I suppose you cannot lament over someone you do not remember or miss.

It made sense. In seminary, we had considered the removal of certain memories as being one of the possibilities in Heaven, but we had dismissed it as being too harsh and unlike God. Now, in my temporary incorruptible tabernacle, it did not seem harsh at all. It seemed reasonable, like it was the only option.

In any event, my focus was on those I knew and was seeing again, and not on those whom I could not recall. The desire to try to re-member those I had forgotten quickly passed, and I enthusiastically greeted family and friends. All the while, I made sure my mother stayed near me.

It was good to sit in that beautiful setting on that wondrous grass and share memories, feeling closer and more connected to these souls than ever I had on Earth. It was clear they felt the same way. There were no tears, no awkward or negative memories, just unrestrained rejoicing in this grand reunion.

I did not feel rushed to end these mini-reunions. In fact, there was no concept of time at all, except in our thoughts and memories of our lives on Earth. While we visited with each other, the cosmic view returned to a position above us. Peeking through the transparent roof of that great hall was the earth, the place we had called home, where yet others we loved and knew still remained.

Previously, I had seen it at my feet through the transparent floor of the first place the angels had brought me. It was puzzling that it was now above me, but I did not let that divert my attention away from the reunion I had looked forward to for so long. It really didn't matter anyway. It seemed fitting for our previous home to be a backdrop for our reunion.

Eventually, the time with family and friends drew to a close and the angels beckoned me to walk down one of the pathways that wound through the grass. They assured me there would be constant fellowship with friends and family in the future, just as there would be constant fellowship with God the Father, but we had to make another stop first. I turned to tell my mother I would return shortly, but she assured me I would not be far away and that we would have all eternity to be together.

I walked the pathway the angels had pointed out to me; they remained behind. The sensation was so much different than walking on Earth had been. There was no feeling of impact or effort. My feet seemed to float. Yet another wondrously new sensation I was sure to enjoy for all time.

To my left I saw movement. As I walked closer to see what it was, I glanced over to my companion angels behind me. They seemed to be smiling as if they were watching me open a gift they had given to me. One said, "More than most, you will appreciate this. We have waited a long time for this moment for you."

Looking back in the direction of the movement, I saw animals— thousands and thousands, perhaps millions and millions of animals. As far as the eye could see there were animals of every variety. There were dogs and cats and every type of pet we knew on Earth. Intermingled with the domestics were the wild animals of Earth— deer, bear, zebra, and any other animal one could name from his or her earthly experience. All were dwelling in peace with the other animals around them.

The impact of what I saw overwhelmed me. The beautiful sight was the validation or proof of all I had taught back on Earth. Although the Bible was very straightforward about the eternal nature of animals, it was satisfying to have visible confirmation.

My faith that God had providentially provided for each of His creatures had been sure and strong, evidenced in my unwavering conviction in the books and articles I had written to help others understand God's providence. But I had often felt so unworthy to carry that message to others that I often doubted myself, not the truth of the message. Seeing animals in Heaven was validation of my work, not the truth of God's care, which had always been sure.

A small group of animals in the section nearest me seemed to momentarily freeze. I heard a little "yip" from deep inside the section and saw one animal making its way toward me. The other animals made way for it, seeming to move in concert to make an open pathway for the one coming toward me.

It was a white dog, and I felt it was one of three white dogs I had shared my life with on Earth. Indeed it was. It was Missy, one of the sweetest, dearest animals God had ever made.

I thought my heart was going to burst with joy. I had missed her so very much. She had lived a long, full life, but it was far too short for me. Her absence in my life had been a continuous burden. She was always on my mind, awake and sleeping.

In fact, on Earth I had vividly dreamed she was still with me. Even the many warts she had had on her tiny little body were present in my dream Missy. As I stirred and awakened, I began to weep. Then it had only been a dream; it had no meaning. But now it was real! She was again with me.

Feeling unsteady from my euphoric state, I knelt down and waited to embrace her. In no time, she was upon me and doing the "Missy dance" that used to make my wife and me chuckle.

She licked my hands and face. I could only utter, "Oh Missy, Missy, I have missed you so much. It has been so hard to go on in life without you. I hope you knew how much you meant to me."

The pleasant surprises in Heaven never seemed to stop. My question had been rhetorical. I hadn't expected an answer.

But Missy answered me. She spoke! In a sweet, childlike voice that was not familiar to me, but that fit her very well. She said, "Of course I knew."

My surprise quickly gave way to elation as I realized another of my teachings had been validated—animals did have the capacity to speak. I had always believed (and taught) that they once had the ability to speak, but lost it when the dread of man came upon them from the curse of mankind's fall. I strongly believed this ability would be restored in the next life. Proof was right there in front of me, in my own Missy girl!

*   *   *

I am going to step out of my insights of Heaven for a moment and speak of my work on Earth. Although I didn't receive a lot of criticism of my work, the idea that animals would speak in Heaven received the lion's share of it and is one teaching I felt needed validation. I do not mean to paint a negative picture, because for every letter or e-mail I received where someone took exception to something I taught, I received thousands of letters of appreciation. Consequently, I never felt unduly ridiculed or challenged.

Still, on Earth, it was difficult for me to understand how anyone could deny the evidences around us regarding the ability of animals to communicate. Our pets often went to great lengths to "talk" with us. The absence of the actual ability to speak in language did not stop them from communicating. They spoke with sounds, body language, and even silly little antics.

Missy, for instance, was born with an overbite. She learned early in life that if she slapped her jaws together it made a snapping sound that we, her human family, found amusing. She quickly learned to use it to get our attention. In fact, it became her signature communications tool. When she wanted something, she would do her little Missy Dance and snap her jaws shut a half dozen times while throwing her head up in the air.

It always got our attention. And once she had our attention, she could communicate what she wanted with other antics she had developed over the years. If she wanted to play ball, it was a simple matter of grabbing it and dropping it at my feet. If she wanted to eat, she would continue her dance and edge toward the kitchen. She had an entire repertoire of signals she sent when she wanted something. And she always got what she asked for.

Our pets "talk" to us all the time. They communicate perfectly what they want. Sometimes all it takes is a certain look in their eyes. Other times they go through a whole process to get us to understand. But they get their messages across.

The reverse is true as well. When we speak to them, they know exactly what *we* want. Through a combination of familiar words, gestures, and tone, they understand. Some are smarter than others, there is no denying that. But they all manage to communicate just the same.

The evidence of animals possessing the ability to speak is documented in Genesis in the account of the serpent talking with Eve in the Garden of Eden. It is not important that the serpent was actually Satan. From Eve's perspective, it was a serpent and she conversed with that serpent in what seems to have been a very natural exchange.

She did not wince or do a double take when the serpent spoke to her. She responded lucidly, without hesitation. That she responded without hesitation shows she was not taken back by an animal speaking. It suggests that talking animals were common in the garden. She viewed the conversation as something rational and normal.

If you were working in your garden and came across a serpent, you probably would show it the business end of a shovel. But if it spoke to you, what then? If it said, "Hey, lighten up. I am keeping the vermin from eating your vegetables," what would you do?

My guess is you would drop the shovel and run quickly in fear. Why would you do that? Because snakes are not supposed to talk! Animals are not supposed to talk. It would be creepy!

If that same dynamic and mind-set existed in the Garden of Eden, Eve would have fled from the presence of the serpent. But she did not do so. Eve did not think it was creepy. She was not shaken. She responded to the serpent as if she had talked with it and the other animals of the garden before. In fact, a short conversation ensued. It seems to have been a routine and natural occurrence.

I believe that in their world of innocence, Adam and Eve spoke regularly with the animals, and the animals spoke back. After all, the animals had been Adam's original and only companions. Companions ordinarily communicate with each other.

Would it be such a long stretch to believe that God made animals with the ability to converse with humans? The animals in Heaven speak to God. Is it not at least within the realm of possibilities that animals spoke with Adam and Eve? I think it not only possible, but quite probable.

Scripture hints at this probability. Numbers, Chapter 22 records the account of the donkey speaking to the prophet Balaam. There are a lot of important spiritual lessons in this account that overshadow the actual act of an animal speaking, but the fact remains, the donkey had the ability to speak. It is prudent to believe the ability was always there, but dormant. When the Lord needed the donkey to speak, the ability was temporarily restored.

As I mentioned above, the beasts around the throne of God worship and praise Him continuously. They do so audibly, speaking words you and I can understand. We are told that they and all the creatures of God will worship the Father and give Him praise.

Evidence is all around us in our world. Some animals have retained the ability to actually speak words, though science says they lack the equipment to do so. Parrots, parakeets, and many other species of birds can mimic human speech. In some cases, they are documented to have used words they have learned in whole sentences, something "dumb animals" are not supposed to be able to do.

Dolphins, apes, and a host of other creatures can and have developed a communication system with humans. The ability to communicate is there. Once they could speak just as you and I. That ability has been temporarily suspended, but will be restored in the future. For the animals that have passed on to the next life, that ability is probably instantly restored.

Sorry for the short rabbit trail. I now will return to my insight of Heaven.

Here was the proof that animals can speak, right in front of me. My Missy was talking to me . . . and acknowledging that she understood when I talked to her back on Earth. She knew how much she meant to me. She knew that we did everything possible to make her life comfortable. She knew that we loved her.

I said, "Oh this is wonderful Missy. How have you been?"

She filled me in on all she had experienced. She cuddled up in my arms the way she did so long ago on Earth and we sat together and talked. I noticed immediately that all the warts that had plagued her previous life were gone. The surgical scars where the largest had been removed were gone as well. Her old eyes were young and bright again. She looked better than she had ever looked.

On Earth, she never complained about her infirmities and I had promised that one day they would be gone and her skin would be renewed. It was so good to see the promise had come true.

She told me that she knew I had enjoyed the popping sound she made when snapping her jaws together, but wanted me to know she was no longer able to do that. Though her new body looked the same, the overbite was gone. That didn't matter to me. Hearing her voice and being able to speak to each other was far better.

She told me that on Earth, she was always aware of what was going on. She knew when I'd had problems at work or when we'd planned a vacation. She knew especially when it was time to go to the veterinarian. She'd always tried to be brave, but did not like going there.

I knew she had understood me back on Earth, but I wanted to know if she had tried to speak to me as well. Her answer was totally unexpected.

"Of course, I tried. I spoke to you all the time, just like I am now. But the words came out as barks and other sounds that did not make sense to you. I did not understand why at that time, but I learned here that was the way things had to be."

"That explains a lot and it is just about the way I suspected it was. Still, it would have been nice to have been able to talk to you like I am now."

Missy suddenly moved to my side, but told me she wouldn't go far. My pets were arriving, and she was simply giving them the chance to reunite with me.

Scooter, my childhood dog, was the next to reach me. After the greetings and pleasantries, he wanted me to know how difficult it had been for him when I grew up and left home to join the Navy. Understanding that I had to leave, had not made it any easier. He'd cherished the times I came home for a visit and how I'd always looked for him first.

He shared with me the first time he saw me and I also recalled it very well. He had been taken from his mother much too soon. He was only eight weeks old. He'd been stuffed into a little cardboard box and put on the floor in the supermarket. At the end of the day, the lights were turned out, and he was so lonely that he cried all night long, but no one came. During the day, he'd felt better because there were people around, but he was still scared and lonely.

He saw me in the store with my mother, and it made him think of his mother who he would never see again. He remembered that I had looked in the box, reached in, and picked him up. He said he hadn't meant to piddle on me, but he was so happy.

When I hugged him, he knew right way that he loved me and could tell that I loved him. He was happy when my mother, after saying "no" so many times, finally gave in and let me buy him as my birthday present. He asked me how much it had cost me to buy him.

I replied, "Only $6.95." I was glad because I had only ten dollars in birthday money.

As we talked about the times we'd had, it was good to know the love we'd held for each other had never waned or flickered.

Scooter moved next to where Missy was and I knew it was time to see yet another of my best friends. Samantha was next. And then

*Pebbles, Odie, Miko, Fuji, and Jello took their turns. I was over-
whelmed. My heart couldn't hold any more joy. Surely it was about
to burst.*

*Each reunion was wonderful as we recounted our lives together
and love for each other. We were a spectacle, jumping for joy and
embracing each other. As we talked, I got to see things from their
perspectives, which were quite revelating. I learned things I had not
known about how they felt about certain things.*

*Pebbles, one of our wonderful, but cowardly Chihuahuas, for
example, revealed she hadn't liked it when I'd played rough with
her. I'd thought she had because she'd tugged on the rope so hard
she'd pulled it out of my hand and rolled backwards.*

*I'd told my wife to "watch this" and sure enough, Pebbles would
tug away. I'd let go of the rope, and over she went. Other times,
I'd pulled pranks on her, like tickle her ear when she was asleep
or turn the windshield wipers on when we drove in the car (she'd
hated those wipers, too), each time, saying, "Watch this!"*

*Over time, Pebbles had learned those words and had become
conditioned to think something bad was going to happen whenever
I said them. Knowing this, I toyed with her. When she was lying
down half asleep, I would say loudly, "Watch this," and Pebbles
would jump up and hide under the nearest piece of furniture in apprehension.*

*I know that sounds mean, but it had not been meant to be cruel.
I did it every so often only for a laugh.*

*In Heaven now, I knew she never liked it. She had not thought
it was funny, and I found myself wishing I had never done it. In
fact, I wished I had spent more time trying to understand all my
pets more.*

Lighthearted laughter occurred when humorous moments were recollected. Samantha and Missy, both Westies, thought it was funny that one loved riding on the lawn tractor with me and hated heights, the other hated the lawn tractor and loved heights.

I had always thought that was funny, too, but wondered how they knew about each other's idiosyncrasies. They had not known each other. Their lives had not overlapped on Earth. Obviously they had discussed it after Missy had passed. It was pleasing to learn they had thought and talked about me.

At some point, I asked, "Who walks you all when you need to go outside?"

My question was met with near hysterical laughter.

All of them laughing at the same time in their child-like voices reminded me of the munchkins laughing in the movie The Wizard of Oz, *but I had no idea why what I said was so funny.*

Missy spoke up. "We don't need to be walked. We could handle that chore ourselves, now, but here, there is no need to be walked."

Well that was a revelation I was not expecting. But it made sense. It occurred to me, even that with all the animals present in that great hall, I hadn't seen one pile of . . . well you know. And I suppose I was pretty happy to know this. It was good to know that I would not have to watch where I stepped.

Fuji, my Siamese, shared some humor with us all. He wished he had listened to me when we moved to Miami and I caught him toying with a scorpion. I'd tried to get it away from him, warning him of the danger, but he had not listened. He'd grabbed it up in his mouth and ran off to continue playing with it. It did not take long until "whammo," it hit him in the upper arm. It was a tough three days for him after that. As touching memory after touching memory was revisited and celebrated, we collectively gave praise to the Lord for our lives together on Earth and the fulfillment of the promise of this blessed reunion. It became clear that my animals were connected to each other as well as to me and that it would remain this way for all eternity. The subdued grief that I had lived with for so many years was gone and in its place was a renewed joyful heart.

I slowly became aware of other gatherings around us. Groups of pets and people were holding their own reunions. I found myself gravitating toward these other groups. I felt connected to them somehow.

My angel escorts assured me that was the way of Heaven. All God's creatures are brought together in fellowship with Him and with each other. All in Heaven have an immediate familiarity with others. There is no conflict, only harmony as the Spirit of God joins our hearts and minds together. "As a result," they explained, "we all feel connected to one another."

It was a very comforting revelation. After all, God is love and the great reconciler. His promise is for peace and harmony and I felt a connection and a harmony with these other groups. I also felt a desire to fellowship with them.

Everywhere I looked, I could see groups of people and animals of varying sizes. Most were about the same size as my own, but some were significantly larger, with hundreds of animals and a dozen or more people. Others were comprised of one or two animals and one person. In each group, animals and people were jumping for joy.

Humans were embracing the pets they had not seen for so many years. Dogs were licking hands and faces, cats were jumping up

*into open arms. Pot belly pigs, horses, ferrets, and a host of other
animals were enjoying their reunions, as well.*

*It was another new experience for me. And I did not hear one
woof or purr. I heard the chatter of what sounded like a thousand
children, excitedly sharing their emotional experiences with others.*

*Above us, birds of every variety and color circled, searching for
their people. Here and there, some landed in groups on the ground.
Birds and parrots of every variety were in abundance. It was a colorful sight, to say the least.*

*One of the birds hovered right in front of me, suspended in the
air as if by some hidden strings or mysterious force. That did not
startle me or confuse me, however. I think I was getting used to
the absence of physics as we knew them on Earth.*

*The bird looked familiar to me, but I could not place it until
she reminded me of how she used to fool me by imitating the ring
of the telephone in our shop in Miami so many years ago. It was
Lola, the African Gray parrot I spoke about in* Cold Noses at the
Pearly Gates.

*I chuckled at the memory, acknowledging that she had indeed
made my life tough with her pranks. She flew off, and I moved
toward the nearest of the groups. Without asking them to do so,
my own pets accompanied me and I realized we would be together
as before, but without fear of separation.*

*As we neared the closest groups we were greeted with cheerful
welcomes and I did not feel as if we were intruding at all. There
were more wagging tails than I had ever seen before and I mused
what a horrendous sound of* thump-thump-thump *there would
have been, had the floor been made of wood.*

A woman emerged from the group and made her way to me. I did not recognize her, but she seemed to know me. She said, "I know you. You wrote that book that helped me so much with my grief. I can't thank you enough." And then she reached out and gave me an unexpected hug.

On Earth, I would have been very embarrassed and uneasy. Recognition always made me uncomfortable. But I felt no discomfort in Heaven. I was changed and rid of the pride that had beset me on Earth. Welcoming the warm display of appreciation, I reminded her that my books merely reflected the promises and provisions made by God. I thanked her and she returned to her group, while I and my pet entourage moved toward one man and a dog.

This man seemed to be more jubilant than any of the others. He was audibly crying out his thanks to God for the reunion. Over and over again, he loudly wailed, "Thank you Lord, Thank you Lord for making him whole again." Big old crocodile tears of joy wetted the fur of the dog he so tightly embraced. Out loud to the Lord, he was expressing his deep gratitude for the wholeness of his best friend.

When I asked what he meant about making his dog whole, he explained that his dog Harley had been the victim of a fatal hit and run that had left him unrecognizable. The man held himself responsible for this terrible tragedy. He had inadvertently left the back yard gate open and his beloved companion had wandered into the street. For weeks, he grieved the dog's passing and felt overwhelming guilt. He confided in me that he had begged God to take care of Harley and make him whole again.

His reunion with Harley overwhelmed him. Not only was the grief lifted, but so too the burden of guilt he had carried for so long. *His joy was too much for him to contain and he had to cry out his gratitude to the Lord.*

I pondered his behavior and came to another realization. Though we are changed to rid us of our self-centeredness and pride, we retain our personalities—that which makes us different from each other—in the next life. Our personality is a reflection of who we are, and this man was just a bit more demonstrative than others.

My attention was drawn to an extraordinarily large group of people and animals. As I drew near, I could see that the people were angels, and they were shuffling the animals toward the other groups.

I turned to the two angels who were accompanying me and asked, "What are they doing?"

One of the angels responded with great compassion, "These are the unwanted and unloved, the abused and forgotten who had no one on Earth. Some are those whose humans will not be here. They are being added to the other groups where they will feel welcome and loved."

Once again, I was overwhelmed by the lovingkindness of God to consider the special needs of these animals that mankind had let down. I couldn't wait for some to be added to our group. Before I could ask when this would happen, I heard the voice of a man behind me.

"Hello. Hello there. We never met, but we communicated with each other on Earth. My name is Bill. I was a pastor when one of my parishioners introduced me to your books. I scoffed and told the woman that animals did not have souls, that when they passed away, that was it, kaput, no more.

"I was so adamant about my beliefs that I felt compelled to

*write to you and put you in your place. You might remember that
I came on hard. I laid into you vehemently and was unbending in
my position."*

I told him that I did not remember him specifically, but I did
recall having several ministers approach me with his same view-
point, some aggressively, some not. Almost invariably, when those
individuals were willing to discuss the matter and look at the Biblical evidence, they usually had a change of mind. In fact, often
they would share their new understandings with their congregations.

"Well, that's just it," he broke in. "I didn't give you a chance
to discuss it with me. I judged you a quack and slammed the door
shut. In fact, I never bothered to read your book. I had it in my
mind that you were totally wrong. Had I read it, I am sure I would
have been at least willing to discuss the matter."

"Well, I suppose it doesn't matter now," I said, "since we are
both here and both know that God does indeed take care of his animals."

He thought for a moment and then nodded "Well, that's just it
you see. I am sorry for having been so narrow-minded and unwill-
ing to consider your conclusions. I let down many in my congrega-
tion by not knowing the facts. You were right. You were absolutely
right. And I must say, I am glad that you were."

"Well thank you," I responded, "but there is no need to apologize. I went many years without knowing the truth of this matter
myself. Only after researching all pertinent Bible passages regarding animals did I come to a firm position."

"Well, thanks again," he offered. "I am sure we will get plenty
of opportunities to revisit this in the future. Right now, I am look-

ing for my own dog, Rosco. I just arrived in the hall and am anxious to see him again."

I gave him a quick hug and told him I would see him again soon. Even that exchange was a new experience for me. I was never a hugger on Earth. I liked shaking hands, but hugging was a little too much for me. But in Heaven, I had no problem with it.

As I moved on, I visited group after group and saw the joyous scene of individual reunions repeated over and over and over again. Everywhere people were giving praise and thanks to the Lord, just as I am sure they did earlier when they were reunited with their human families.

More people and animals were arriving from Earth all the time. It seemed to be a continuous celebration and reunion. From every corner of the great hall praises were offered up to God for the joy that was being experienced. The praises seemed to rise up and join together in a chorus. It was so pure and sincere, undoubtedly a sweet savor to the Lord.

Now, please don't misunderstand. All animals, as indeed all people and angels, belong to God. Their allegiance and devotion is to Him, as is mine. But our time of fellowship and devotion to God will be spent together with those we loved and knew on Earth.

I had not had that understanding. My notion or opinion had been that while special memories of and connections to those we shared our lives with on Earth existed, our focus and attention would be on God alone.

Clearly, I had assumed too much. God apparently had other plans, better plans, and I was thankful that He did. I would not be separated again from my pets or my mother and others of my family.

In Heaven, I recalled moments of great joy experienced on Earth—the birth of my children, time spent with my grandchildren, and especially my marriage to a wonderful woman. I remembered those unforgettable moments of happiness made all the toil and trouble of life seem worth the struggle. But they were only moments. Time had a way of robbing much of the thrill. That joy was earthly and fleeting.

The joy that flooded over me in Heaven was different. It was lasting. It was pure. It was not a high point in a life of toil, but a steady feeling of elation with no fear that it would ever end. It found companionship with the joy of other souls of God's creation. Our individual joys meshed together to form a collective super joy, if you will, basking in the presence of the majesty of the Almighty and the place He had prepared for us.

I now return to the here and now to bring this chapter to a close. I know that this topic of animals having eternal souls is not an essential or major doctrine of the Bible. I know that the theme of the Bible, both Old and New Testament, is the revelation of God's son to mankind and the focus of that revelation is the reconciliation of mankind with God.

In that sense, the providential and eternal care for animals by God did not rise to a very high level of importance. Indeed, whether we humans know about or acknowledge God's provision for His animals has no impact on the fact that He loves and preserves them. Our ignorance or unbelief has no impact on the fact that God promised and purposed to take care of these personalities we call animals and that he will fulfill that promise.

But thankfully, He said enough in His Word for us to know this truth, because having that knowledge is important to us. To know that God made these creatures eternal, just as He did the angels and humans; to know that He tells us they are "safe" in His hands; and to know they will enjoy eternity with us in Heaven is a comfort to those of us who have invested our time and love in their earthly care.

Whether they precede or follow us to this place, we are guaranteed a grand and lasting reunion with them. They, like us, will be renewed and given incorruptible, eternal bodies free from illness or ailment. They will be given the faculties to communicate and converse with us and we will share an eternity together in fellowship with and worship of the one who created us all.

The joy will be unprecedented to anything we have experienced before. There shall be no waning of that high emotional feeling of contentment, not even after ten thousand years. As the old hymn tells us, "After ten thousand years we will have just begun . . ."

We shall not age or pass away. We shall never experience a bad moment or drop tears of grief. Neither shall our animals. All of God's creatures will live abundantly and eternally in His blessed presence.

That brushes only the surface of the wonder of the place called Heaven. The half of what awaits us has not been told, indeed cannot be told, for God has written ". . . eye hath not seen, nor ear heard, neither have entered into the heart of man, the things which God hath prepared for them that love Him"(I Corinthians 2:9). We are given a partial glimpse of what He has prepared for us. Like that part of the iceberg that we cannot see, so much more good and blessing is hidden from our view. But it is there and He will reveal it in His time.

For now, we must be satisfied with the glimpses He gives us. The reunion with family and friends, human and animal is sure. It is sure, because we can trust what God has written and promised. The promises of God are sure. His Word is the only true constant in this life. He is faithful to His promises and what He has written will come to pass.

Let us summarize the promises or glimpses He has given us in terms of what the next life will be like for our pets.

First, we know our animals are not bodies with souls, but souls with bodies. and we know that the soul is eternal. God promises that in His capable and almighty hands "is the soul of every living thing" (Job 12:10). Our pets do not pass away. Rather, they pass on ahead. A subtle play on words, but with huge eternal ramifications.

Next, we know that when they pass on ahead, they are restored or renewed, just as humans who have reconciled with God are promised to be. The ills of their earthly flesh are left behind and they are given new, youthful bodies without blemish or ailment.

While in this place without time, they do not wait, pining away in unhappiness. They are in the presence and majesty of their Creator and fear and longing no longer exist. They are undoubtedly conscious of the love they have for us, but because time does not exist, the years it takes for us to join them in that blessed place seem like but moments to them.

Finally, we are assured of a reunion. In fact, we will have many reunions on that distant glorious shore. Of utmost priority and importance is our meeting with our Father God. The Bible says in Romans Chapter 8 ". . . the whole creation groans and travails in pain . . ." waiting on the great day of meeting the Lord God. Everything in creation, even creation itself, is driving toward this reunion with the Creator.

That reunion subordinates all other reunions. In our flesh, we may not perceive it that way, but it will be the most significant individualized event in the life of all who have been created. Again in Romans Chapter 8 we are told, "For I reckon that the sufferings of this present time are not worthy to be compared with the glory which shall be revealed in us."

The hymn "When We See Jesus" says, "It will be worth it all, when we see Jesus; life's trials will seem so small, when we see Christ. . . ." This then will be that day of reunion, when the created meets the Creator face-to-face.

Following that will be the reunion we have with family and friends; human and animal. It will be a wonderful time, a much anticipated time, and an unforgettable time. The corruptness and injustices of Earth will be far behind. The fears and doubts we struggled with will have been dispatched and our faith will have been turned into sight. Unencumbered by time or schedule, the reunion will not be rushed in the hustle-bustle ways of Earth. It will be a reuniting, one that shall last for all eternity.

Chapter 9

THE RAINBOW BRIDGE

Just about anyone who has lost a pet and has access to a computer has read or at least heard of the poem "The Rainbow Bridge." This anonymous poem speaks of a bridge in Heaven where pets wait for their people to arrive. It touches and soothes the grieving and captures the hopes of those who have lost a beloved family pet and best friend.

Several hundred kindhearted readers have shared copies of this poem with me over the years. I appreciate their thoughtfulness for taking the time to send me something that was so moving and helpful to them.

Invariably, they also had questions about the poem. They wanted to know what I thought of the poem. Is it true? Is it accurate? Is there such a bridge mentioned in the Bible? They also wanted to know if I thought their best friend would be waiting there for them. Less often, but enough times to be flattering, I have been asked if I was the anonymous author of this touching poem. I would like to share my answers to their questions as a help for others who might have the same concerns.

First, I am definitely not the author of this poem. It may reflect, as some have pointed out, the same compassion readers find in my books, but I assure you, this poem is not my work. My research reveals the poem was first published somewhere in the mid to late 1980s. I did not author my first book, *Cold Noses at the Pearly Gates*, until 1996. Prior to that, the only real writing I had done was technical publications for the United States Coast Guard and an article for *Proceedings*, a magazine published by the U. S. Naval Institute.

To help me answer the other questions about the bridge and whether our pets are waiting there, I have included the original poem for your reference and convenience. Unfortunately, there are no less than a dozen versions of this poem floating around the Internet, and quite possibly, many more. Determining which version was the original proved to be an arduous and impossible task.

However, this tidbit of information might interest you. I actually found it quite humorous. I discovered that although the poem is widely accepted to be anonymous, almost all of the versions I located had copyrights attached to them with strict warnings against reproduction. Ironically, it appears that even the true author would not be allowed to make copies of his or her own work if they were inclined to obtain a copy.

Though I could not determine which version was the original, all is not lost. Here is the version that seems to be more prolific on the Internet than all the others combined. Coincidentally, it is also the version that readers send to me most frequently. And thankfully, it is not encumbered with the same copyright warnings attached to others.

The fact that it always appears with "Author Unknown" at the bottom suggests that it may be the original, but of course, we cannot be sure. In any event, this version captures the essence of all the other versions and will serve our purpose.

The Rainbow Bridge

Just this side of heaven is a place called the Rainbow Bridge.

When an animal dies that has been especially close to someone here, that pet goes to the Rainbow Bridge.

There are meadows and hills for all of our special friends so they can run and play together.

There is plenty of food, water and sunshine, and our friends are warm and comfortable.

All the animals who had been ill and old
*   are restored to health and vigor;*
those who were hurt or maimed are made whole and strong again,
*   just as we remember them in our dreams of days*
*   and times gone by.*
The animals are happy and content, except for one small thing;
*   they each miss someone very special to them, who*
*   had to be left behind.*
They all run and play together, but the day comes
*   when one suddenly stops and looks into the distance.*
His bright eyes are intent; his eager body quivers.
*   Suddenly he begins to run from the group,*
flying over the green grass,
*   his legs carrying him faster and faster.*

You have been spotted,
  and when you and your special friend finally meet,
you cling together in joyous reunion, never to be parted again.
The happy kisses rain upon your face;
  your hands again caress the beloved head,
  and you look once more into the trusting eyes of your pet,
so long gone from your life but never absent from your heart.
Then you cross the Rainbow Bridge together. . . .

—Author unknown

Regarding the origins of the poem, my best guess is that it was authored by someone who had lost a dear and cherished pet and who was also acquainted with Norse legends and folklore, in particular, the legend of Bifrost. Attempting to console themselves they adapted the legend to include animals, and specifically, family pets.

Bifrost, in Norse mythology, is the bridge between the realm of mankind, called Midgard, and the realm of the Norse gods, Asgard. The bridge is described differently in various writings, but generally the bridge is said to be encased in supernatural flame and is comprised of many colors, which is where the rainbow reference apparently comes from.

Though it has no bearing on this study, it is interesting to note that the remains of exceedingly large humanoids found around the world are often connected to this same legend. The bones, usually of individuals eight feet tall or greater, are alleged to be those of ancient Vikings or Norsemen. Apparently, the mythical bridge was used by mythical giants to enter this world.

Of course, I cannot be sure of my assumption that the poem about the Rainbow Bridge came about as a result of someone with knowledge of this legend applying the myth to animals. But that is not a concern for me as you will see with my answers to the other questions.

I can say without hesitation or reservation that the Rainbow Bridge is not real. It is simply a myth. It is definitely not mentioned in the Bible and is not part of the Heaven of the Bible. Those are my quick answers and I know they will not sit well with everyone. My hope is that you will read my more considered response in the following paragraphs. I am sure you will find my reasoning lucid and convincing. Hopefully, it will also be comforting.

While I admit the poem is pleasant, generally comforting and has no doubt helped many an ailing heart, it simply is not Biblical. One of the most critical elements of the Christian hope is that God promised that Heaven will be nothing like Earth. All the pain and suffering, death and sorrow, unfairness and injustice—those things of Earth—will not be present or found in Heaven. They will be left behind.

It is inconceivable then that our animals could sit sadly waiting for our arrival. If they could be sad, what would be different from Earth? What would be the reason to go there if things there were the same as here? The most potent, persuasive, and promising thing about Heaven is that it will be a place of bliss without regret, pining, or sadness.

What would happen to those hapless creatures waiting on the bridge if their people did not make it to Heaven? Oh my, that is one eventuality the poet did not take into consideration. Would the animals remain there, suffering forever? Doesn't sound like much of a Heaven to me.

The fact that the bridge is not Biblical is not my only objection. There is another failing in this poem. It makes the assumption that the animals that have passed continue to belong to us. While a special bond between us and the animals we shared our lives with will undoubtedly exist forever, there can be no doubt that they belong to God. We are given temporary dominion over them and charged with caring for them. We develop relationships with them and love them. But ultimately and rightfully, they belong to their creator.

I do not dislike the poem. I know it has helped many. But when it comes to eternity, only the Bible can offer insight we can trust and place our confidence in, not anonymous poetry. A poem that captures the promises of God and the reality of Heaven should be Biblically based, such as the following.

REUNION MEADOW

In innocence you were formed,
  A loving and living soul
Entrusted to man's care;
  Your presence made him whole.
By his error and not your own,
  You suffered from his fall;
His fate became yours,
  As death doth claim us all.
No matter that result,
  You lived your life for man

A noble, devoted creature;
  Alongside him you ever ran;
You cared for his flocks,
  Protected family and home,
Licked his hand in love
  When given only a bone,
Or purred warmly for the ones
  Who opened their hearts and their home,
Who in your eyes was your all and all,
  No matter the damage done by their fall.
Never turning on the hand you loved
  Never aware of the life that waits above,
Giving your all to the one you served,
  Never receiving all you deserved,
Passing from their blessed care
  To where most know not where
Leaving with promise to see you again
  But uncertain of how or where or when.
But in that place of forevermore,
  Just beyond the heavenly shore,
Lies a meadow of blues and silvers and golds
  Where are kept in peace God's innocent souls:
There his creatures live in promised bliss
  With no care of an earthly someone missed;
When comes that day of grand reunion,
  They will then remember their cherished human.

                                —*Gary Kurz*

I hope learning that the Rainbow Bridge poem is not only anonymous, but fictitious will not cause you any despair. The promises of God regarding the animals He created and loves are so much more potent in terms of their eternal welfare. On the fabled bridge they would pine away for who knows how long waiting for their person to show. For those whose person would never show, despair would be grievously unbearable. How could this be considered a place of happiness and rest?

In the hands of the Almighty, they will not pine or despair. They will enjoy immediate wholeness and happiness, which would increase exponentially when their person arrived, but would not wane at all if they did not. Regardless, the point is that they will be happy in any circumstance and not sitting unfulfilled and unhappy on some mythical bridge.

Chapter 10

FINAL THOUGHTS

A s we have seen, Heaven is a wonderful place. For those of us who have lost cherished pets, it is comforting to know they enjoy the splendor of that place right now. By virtue of the fact that they are innocent creatures, with no need of reconciliation they pass from this world to the next without judgment or delay.

This is the way their creator planned it. This is His will. Knowing this does little to ease the pain of one's loss, but it does eliminate the fear of wondering or speculating what becomes of our best friend's precious soul. To know they are happy at this very moment is a comfort in the midst of our pain.

Still, that knowledge does not answer all the questions people have at traumatic times. Matters of the heart still need answers. For instance, I am often asked why a person grieves the passing of their pet so deeply. Readers express a feeling of guilt for having mourned their pet more than they had the passing of a close relative. I realize they are looking for justification of those feelings as much as an answer to why this occurs, and I am happy to try to provide both if I am able.

Knowing the intricacies of each individual situation is nearly impossible, of course. Even when readers write lengthy introductions and explain the situations they have endured, it is difficult for me to know all the facts in order to give them the answers they seek. I cannot take the cookie-cutter approach. It is too important to the reader and each case must receive customized attention.

But generally speaking, there are some easy to understand causes for people feeling such trauma over the passing of their best friends. For one thing, few things in life give us as much satisfaction as when we are loved and appreciated. When we know we are important to someone else and are foremost in and on their minds, we have a deep sense of worth and purpose. Our pets make us feel cherished, not just loved.

Pets often "light up" when they see us. They express their love without reservation. It is impossible for them to mask or hide the sincerity of how they feel. They don't even try. They are very demonstrative—prancing, dancing, jumping, and kissing wildly.

With family, sometimes even close family, relationships are often more obligatory and forced than sincere. I am not saying that is always the case. Some families are very close and are quite demonstrative, but not all. Animals are open about their love and express it boldly. There is no obligation on their part. Their love is never feigned.

Sadly, human love is often fickle and conditional. It is also fleeting and can end unexpectedly at any time, and for a variety of reasons. That is not the case with the family pet. Okay, maybe we can't say that wholeheartedly about cats without chuckling. They certainly epitomize fickleness, but are still loyal and loving. There is no pretense with them. You always know where you stand. You exist to cater to their needs and they graciously love you in return for doing so.

No matter, pets of every type bring their humans great joy. Dogs, cats, parrots, horses, pot belly pigs, monkeys, ferrets, and a host of other animals offer us love and devotion without condition and make us feel special. They accept us with all our infirmities and faults. Their only desire is to be near us. They don't care if we haven't bathed, if we smoke, if we are Democrat or Republican, or if we are mad at the world, just so long as they can be near us.

That is not the only reason we love them so dearly. On another level, our pets are like perpetual children. Children, because like human offspring, they depend upon us for all their needs—shelter, sustenance, safety, companionship, and well-being. Perpetual because unlike human children, they never grow up and move away. They do not go off to college. They do not join the military. They do not get married. They remain our "children" for the duration of their lives.

Our human relatives are usually in charge of their own lives. They live apart from us, make their own decisions, and provide for themselves. We feel no obligation and have virtually no control over their lives. With our pets, it is completely different. We are obligated to them, but we willingly accept that obligation. For all their lives, for all their needs, we are there for them.

So when they pass, it is more than just losing someone we love and who loves us. We feel that somehow we have let them down. They depended upon us for everything in life and ultimately, because we could not prevent their passing, we failed them. At least that is what is going on in our minds.

The cold, hard fact is that we have no control over life—not theirs, not our own. We cannot add one additional second to our own lives, nor can we add to theirs. Knowing that does not help eliminate our feeling of guilt. We hold ourselves in a sort of self-loathing contempt. They looked to us in time of need and we have always answered the call. But in their most difficult hour, we could do nothing to help them.

If you find yourself feeling this way, there is something you can do to help yourself. Instead of blindly accepting the guilt trip you have, take an honest look at the facts. Ask yourself some difficult questions, putting yourself on trial, so to speak, to determine if you are guilty of some wrong doing or failure.

Did you do everything possible to help your best friend? By that, I mean did you do everything you knew to do? Don't blame yourself if your pet had some undiscovered medical condition you feel you should have known about. How should you have known about it? How could you have known about it?

Don't blame yourself if your best buddy dug a hole under the backyard fence and ran away or got hit by a car. How could you have foreseen that? It is not reasonable to hold yourself responsible for things that are not within your control.

Here is another question you might ask yourself. If you had been able to do anything else, would you have done it? If some new treatment that could have saved your cat cost $1,000, would you have spent it? If you had been able to do anything to help him/her, would you have done it?

If the answer to these questions is "yes," as I suspect they are, then release yourself from your self-condemnation. It is undeserved. I know (and so do you), that if there had been anything you could have done, up to and including risking your own life, you would have done it. But it was all out of your control, and if you have no control, there is no room or justification for blame or guilt.

What I am about to say may cause you to tear up a little and for that I am truly sorry, but I think it will help to hear it. I think it might ease any residual feelings of guilt you may have.

Again, I do not mean to cause anyone additional pain. My motive is to help only. The Bible says "Faithful are the wounds of a friend" (Proverbs 27:6). In other words, a friend won't shade or hide the truth. They will tell you the truth even if it hurts, because they care about you.

For instance, if you are wearing something that looks silly or out of place, someone who is not a friend might say, "Oh, it looks okay," because they really don't care about you as a friend. They don't want the hassle of telling you the truth and possibly having you upset at them.

But a friend will tell you that your clothes look silly in order to save you embarrassment. They expose themselves to your ire because they care about you and how you might feel if you go out in public looking silly.

So, in the spirit of friendship, this truth might cause you some pain, but you need to hear it in order to put your emotions into the proper context. My aim is not to bring you pain, but to help you look at your guilt from a different and more appropriate perspective.

This is the truth I want to share. I truly believe that if your best friend could contact you right now and speak to you, they would say something like, "Please don't blame yourself for my passing. It was my time and nothing you or I could have done could have changed it. I am so thankful my life was spent with you. I am so happy you opened your heart and home and took me in and showered me with love and care. Thank you for loving me. Thank you so much. I am in a place of more love and happiness and one day I will be able to share this with you. Until then, be happy for me in this place and do not blame yourself in any way."

Again, I am sorry if those thoughts hurt you, but I think it is very important we understand that the guilt we feel is false and unfounded. The truth is, we have much to be lauded for regarding our love and care for our pets. If there is any guilt to be assigned, it would belong to the woeful, unjust, and unforgiving world in which we live.

The world we occupy is a complete aberration from what God intended it to be. It is a world fallen out of fellowship with God and into immorality, injustice, suffering, sorrow, and death. Everything that comprises this world is in some state of decay or deterioration.

But not so this place called Heaven. The Lord tells us in Matthew 6:20 that it is a place ". . . where neither moth nor rust doth corrupt." There is no deterioration, no decay. We are told it is a world where there is no fear, pain, illness, want, anguish, sin, sorrow, or death. It is a place of true, abundant, and whole-some life that neither wanes nor fails.

This is where your best friend is. There is nothing to mourn except his or her absence in your life. That is understandable, of course, but that pain should be offset by the knowledge that he/she is enjoying all this new home has to offer, which we have already adequately addressed in other chapters.

Mourn not those who have gone on ahead. They are benefit-ted richly beyond anything you or I could have done for them. It is difficult to grieve the passing of the caterpillar when one be-holds the beauty of the emerging butterfly unfurling its wings. Essentially, that is what the next or new life is, a putting off of the old, encumbered life, and taking on the new life free from the things of Earth that beset us and weigh us down.

Heaven is a real and wonderful place. It is many things to be sure, but one of the most important truths for pet people is that it is a place of reunion. Comfort yourself with the knowledge that one day you shall see your best friend again.

Chapter 11

MOVING, HUMOROUS, AND THRILLING STORIES
(About Animals and People)

When I first started writing, I included my e-mail address in everything I wrote, if it were possible. Some media outlets did not allow for this, so I included the URL to my website, where people could find my personal contact information.

I knew many readers would have additional questions or need clarification on topics I had covered and felt it was my responsibility to be available to help when I could. My writings, though classified by the media world as being of the "How to" genre, were actually meant to be a support resource for grieving pet owners. It seemed prudent that I provide follow-up help for anyone seeking it.

Editors, marketing people, and even other authors I knew and had worked with called it a foolish idea. They predicted I would be inundated with e-mail from less than stable individuals, perhaps even stalked, because it was a fairly easy process to discover the physical address of someone via their e-mail address. They maintained that it was a bad idea and that it just was not done in the industry.

I struggled with whether to do it or not. I was concerned about safety, not for myself, but for my family. I am big and strong and just dumb enough to think I can take care of anyone seeking to do me harm. In my mind, that's a formidable combination for any stalker to face. But again, I did not want to put my family at risk.

Eventually, I put those fears to rest and made the decision to go against popular opinion. I included my e-mail address for readers whenever I could. It may not have been a wise decision, but it turned out to be a very good one. In fifteen years of writing, I have had more than thirty thousand readers contact me for support. Some had additional questions. Others were just seeking a friend to help with their grief.

I cannot tell you how grateful I am to have been trusted by these folks to help in their hour of need. I answered every e-mail personally and spent as much time as needed to help. The feeling of satisfaction I gleaned from this work was humbling and I thank God every day that I made the right decision. Though each contact came as a result of loss and grief, and I mourned with each reader, it was a pleasure to be of service to them.

In case you are wondering, yes, there were some negative experiences, but they were very few, relatively speaking. One fellow contacted me to ask why I had moved from Houston (I had moved to Kansas). He had driven all the way from Ohio to meet me.

That wasn't scary as some might imagine it could have been. He was on vacation in the area at the time and sounded pretty stable. But then, you never know. In any event, I was glad that I had moved and did not share with him the address of my new home.

The one thing I did not anticipate, however, was telephone calls. It seems in this age of fingertip technology, anyone can find you and your telephone number, even when it is unlisted. I received a handful of telephone calls from very distraught people. When I realized their emotional state, I was happy to spend the two or three hours on the telephone that generally was needed to bring them a sense of peace. I only wish they had checked the time zone differences before they called. They never erred in my favor.

No matter these small inconveniences, nothing but positive benefits came from posting my e-mail address. Readers had an additional resource of help, I had a feeling of being useful to others, and I made many new friends. Additionally, I was able to collect substantial data from a vast and diverse group of pet loving people to pass along in other books and articles.

From the many readers who contacted me after reading *Cold Noses at the Pearly Gates*, I was able to identify additional needs that I addressed in the next book, *Wagging Tails in Heaven*. I would have never guessed that my desire to help people would pay the extra dividend of them helping me, but it did.

Communications from readers were easily 99.99 percent positive. They provided validation that my research was helpful to others and confirmation that my decision to give out my personal contact information was a good one. Readers have been so very kind. They have graciously lauded my work and heaped unsolicited verbal and written accolades upon me, none of which I deserve.

I cannot express strongly enough how much I appreciate each and every one who contacted me, even the three o'clock in the morning telephone callers. Pet people are by far some of the warmest and kindest souls.

Contact with readers turned out to be quid quo pro. Not only did I give them support and a listening ear, but they gave me feedback and an opportunity to discern what the majority of those contacting me wanted addressed next. I was happy to accommodate them and address their concerns from a Biblical point of view.

One of the surprising by-products (at least to me) to come from the many contacts was the knowledge that readers liked the stories I sprinkled into each chapter. In particular, they liked the chapters dedicated solely to stories.

The questions asked most about my stories were "Is that true?" or "Did that really happen?" I always answered in the affirmative, because all of my stories are either from true-to-life personal experiences or things I have read about from reputable news sources. I never embellish or fudge on the facts.

Before I released *Wagging Tails in Heaven*, I announced its production via several Internet forums. Many readers contacted me and asked if I was going to include more stories. I was flattered to know that candid snapshots of my experiences were well-received and felt that I had no choice but to accommodate their requests.

For this outing, more readers asked for stories to be included. In fact, several asked if I would add more than the customary six or seven stories that I have included in the past. I am only too happy to accommodate those requests. I have no shortage of tales to tell, and I love telling them.

So, the following stories are offered in direct response to the requests of readers. Thank you for showing an interest and for asking for more. I hope you find them interesting and humorous. Some are tear-jerkers, a few are scary, perhaps harrowing, and others are just plain amusing. But all are true. I guarantee it.

I understand many who will be reading this book have recently experienced a personal loss and probably do not need to read anything sad. Accordingly, I will place an asterisk (★) next to the tear-jerker stories so you can skip over them if you prefer.

SAILORS GO APE AT ZOO

"Come on, come on," one of the sailors urged the gorilla. "Pick it up, pick it up." He and his two buddies were poised and ready for a tug of war with the big female gorilla at the Honolulu Zoo. They looked hot in their dress uniforms on that typically hot and humid summer day on Oahu as they tried to coax the 350 pound ape into competition.

The enclosure had been constructed with a three foot length of three-inch plastic piping suspended between the inner and outer fences of the exhibit. A six foot piece of very heavy rope ran through the pipe. Approximately three feet of slack allowed the rope to move easily when pulled from either end, but the knots at each end prevented it from being pulled through the pipe. Daring visitors could have a tug of war with the female gorilla—if they so desired.

Apparently, the gorilla had long since tired of the game as the sailors were having little success in getting her attention. I wondered why they had not set this apparatus up at the larger male gorilla's cage. He was much more aggressive than the female and I was sure he would respond more readily to such coaxing.

I did not linger on that question as I was preoccupied with watching the sailors make their unsuccessful bid to interest the female. They tried everything from taunting her with harsh words to mocking her with their renditions of a gorilla beating its chest, to even a very poor Tarzan yell. Nothing seemed to work. The old girl just sat quietly on her behind gazing off into space.

The sailors were clearly tiring in their attempts. They decided to give up. They relaxed their ready stance, threw the rope down in disgust and started to walk away. Without warning, the gorilla came to life. She quickly moved over to where her side of the rope was hanging. I had a feeling she had been baiting them.

Seeing her unexpected interest, the sailors let out a collective gleeful squeal and turned back to the rope, which they grabbed, readying once again their competitive stance. It was obvious that she was good at this game. She was playing them like a fiddle. They reacted just as she wanted them to.

She sat still and did not move. Perhaps fifteen or twenty seconds went by before one of the sailors grew impatient and yelled, "Come on you stupid gorilla!" In the blink of an eye, the gorilla grabbed her end of the rope and tugged hard with one arm. She didn't stand. She did not grasp the rope with two hands. She didn't even brace herself. She simply grabbed the rope with her right hand and jerked it sharply.

It was enough. In fact, it was more than enough. The sailors, who I would guess had a combined weight of at least a hundred pounds greater than that of the gorilla, were lifted off the ground and literally smashed into their side of the fence. To me, it looked like a cartoon where someone's shoes are left standing where they once stood. They didn't lose their shoes, but they might as well have. They lost everything else—the tug of war, their dignity, and the interest of the gorilla—as she turned and went back to her former place of vigil.

The sailors were visibly shaken. I don't think they expected the gorilla to be that powerful. I know I didn't. She was amazingly strong and extraordinarily patient. I remember being thankful the sailors had let go of the rope as quickly as they had. I was sure she would have pulled them right through that three-inch pipe if they hadn't.

I also understood why the tug of war had not been erected at the male gorilla's cage.

Sharks Just Need a Hug, Too

Before I start this story, I want you to know that I have matured considerably since the time this took place. I have sought for some way to make this small slice of my early life sound good, but without success. It is not possible. What I did was foolish at every level and at any age. I will just swallow my pride and own up to having been completely insane when I was young.

When I was ten years old, I lived in Key West, Florida, and spent almost all my time in or on the ocean. On this particular day, I was snorkeling on the southern side of Key West in the

Atlantic Ocean with a man by the name of Mark Hellinger. He was the son of the late Hollywood producer and director of the same name. He was also a close friend of my parents.

Mark was an oddball character. He had inherited millions of dollars from his father's estate and had spent it more quickly than most of us would think possible. He was very generous and gave much away to his friends . . . his adult friends. I never got any, but then as a kid, money wasn't very important to me.

My parents told me that Mark had also inherited another large fortune from an aunt, which he also managed to go through in short order. To say he was irresponsible would be an injustice. He was carefree and not overly concerned with being wealthy.

He was kind of a hero to me. He took me fishing and snorkeling whenever he had time and also let me into the movie theater where he worked, free of charge. He was the projectionist and if I remember correctly, part owner as well.

We were snorkeling in water about eight feet deep, having a great time catching, examining, and releasing sea horses and horseshoe crabs, catching southern lobsters, and generally just having a great time about a quarter mile off shore. That may sound like a long distance from shore, but the water is very shallow on that side of Key West and deepens very gradually.

We happened upon a cement pipe about twelve feet long and perhaps a yard in diameter. It appeared to be a length of sewer piping. How it got there is anyone's guess. Mine would be that it was probably lost off a barge of some sort, though it was rather shallow for a barge to have been there. Perhaps it had been scuttled out in deeper water and storm surges had moved it to that location over the years. Who knows?

Apparently, the pipe had been there for some time, because it was literally covered with seaweed and barnacles. Scores of small fish darted in and out of the cracks in the pipe. I chased after one and peered into the crack where it had disappeared. I was startled by something large moving inside the pipe. I could not make out what it was so I motioned for Mark to come over to take a look. He saw the movement, too.

He moved quickly to one end of the pipe to look inside. I was not far behind. We strained to adjust our eyes to the sudden darkness, and in a few moments we were able to see. What we saw gave us such a start that we surfaced quickly in panic. Inside the pipe, was a large shark, perhaps seven or eight feet long.

We were sure that it was a relatively harmless nurse shark, but Mark wanted to make sure so he shared a quickly concocted plan with me. We would each go to an end of the pipe to cover both entrances. Once in position, whoever was at the tail end of the shark, would prod it with their spear to make it exit the pipe. The one on the other end would then try to grab it as it came out.

I bet you have already guessed which end I got. In retrospect, I think Mark probably arranged it that way. But I didn't care. Hey, I was ten. It sounded like a great plan to me!

We got to our respective ends of the pipe at just about the same time. I looked in the pipe and figured out very quickly that my side of the pipe had been "heads." I was staring at the biggest mouthful of teeth I had ever seen. There must have been a thousand jagged teeth going every which way in that shark's mouth. Well, that is my memory anyway.

But that was not the worst of it. As I strained my eyes, I could see around the sides of the shark to the lighted opening on the other side. There I saw Mark with his spear arm drawn back ready to do the prodding. For just a brief moment it occurred to me that maybe this wasn't such a great idea. This fish was going to be plenty mad when Mark poked it and that mouthful of teeth was coming my way.

How I wished I had thought of that a moment earlier. But alas, that moment was gone. Mark delivered the blow to the shark's tail and, as expected, it came flying out of the opening headed right for me. All I could think to do was to tackle it like Mark had told me to.

As I lunged at it with an underwater bear hug, that fish hit me with a force I had not anticipated. It knocked my mask off, knocked the wind out of me, and bowled me backwards and down into the coral like a little rag doll. It scraped me along the coral floor a little bit longer than it probably needed to. I think it was just trying to teach me a lesson. Fortunately, though in considerable pain and discomfort, I knew it had not taken a bite out of me.

Years later as a surfer in Hawaii, I would experience that feeling of being jammed into the coral many times, but then it would be the expected result of falling off my board. At age ten, I had every expectation that I was going to wrestle that critter into submission, so being pile driven into the sand and coral was a big surprise.

I have no idea why it had not bitten me, but I was very thankful that it had not. I was cut up a bit and bruised from the coral, but I was okay. Mark pulled me up to the surface because I was struggling to get my wind back. I expected him to be upset that

I had not been successful, but he seemed to genuinely appreciate the halfhearted attempt I had made.

So my idol was happy, I was alive, the shark got away, and I had a whopper of a tale to tell. It had been a good day.

⋆ "SHACKLES" THE DOG, A MILITARY HERO

"Chief, this is a hot one," I somehow managed to say in a quivering voice as I choked back tears. "Please stop what you are doing and get this message out to the fleet, top priority".

"Aye, aye sir," came the customary nautical acknowledgment as the Chief grabbed the message and hurried off in the direction of the Communications Center.

After only a few steps, however, apparently having read the first few lines of the message, Chief Petty Officer Smith stopped suddenly in his tracks and turned back toward me in disbelief. His mouth opened, but he didn't say anything. He didn't have to. I knew what he was thinking and solemnly nodded my head in understanding.

Composing himself, he turned back around and headed again toward the Communications Center. The message would be electronically forwarded to major Coast Guard units in a matter of minutes for further dissemination to smaller units. Soon everyone would know.

I glanced again at my copy of the message I had just received from one of our isolated stations in the South Pacific. The Officer in Charge was sending the sad news that Seaman Shackles had passed away during the night. He wasn't really a seaman. He wasn't even a person. He was a Labrador retriever . . . a dog, but a very special dog. He had been the cherished mascot of a Coast Guard Loran Station for over a decade.

Most of the two hundred plus Coast Guard operational shore units are staffed with a "station dog" like Shackles. This unofficial member of the crew is usually "enlisted" from a local shelter and made an honorary member of the crew. Breed and gender are not important. The only prerequisite for the job is an affinity to love and be loved.

To this end, the station dog must be able to stand up to constant pampering and endure massive amounts of stroking and hugs. Once onboard the base, the station dog must also work like any other member of the crew, albeit at somewhat less demanding duties.

He/she must patrol the compound (in search of handouts); escort emergency crews to their response boats (for a pat on the head); and enthusiastically greet those coming on watch (to conduct an olfactory once-over of their lunch bags). As a member of the crew, the station dog is at liberty to dig holes, jump in vehicles with muddy feet, and borrow the only softball during a scheduled off-duty game with impunity.

They are first in line at chow, last to settle down for the night, and enjoy amnesty for anything chewed, buried, or soiled. Generally, they are the best fed and most pampered animals on the planet, but they earn those privileges. They render a service no other crewmember can provide. They make a station a home.

Shackles earned his privileges. He was eleven human years old when he passed, but during his short life he built a legacy that would far outlive him. Hundreds of sailors had been stationed at this isolated outpost during Shackles lifetime and he had befriended them all. In the days when e-mail and cell phones were nothing more than growing ideas in the minds of electronic engineers, families were not just a push of a button away.

Often mail would take a month to arrive. Dogs like Shackles played a critical role as companion and friend. It was common for sailors to become lonely and homesick on that little strip of land in the middle of the ocean. Many found a piece of home in Shackles. He wanted to be everyone's friend. If you were lonely, if you needed a friend, he was your boy. He always had time for you.

Without realizing the role he played, Shackles made life on the island bearable for many. One could run up the beach with this loving communal canine and forget, at least temporarily, that they missed home. Over the years he had impacted hundreds of lives in just this way. All of them had come and gone, but he remained.

Sailors were honored with military decorations and great fanfare for their year-long sacrifice, but not Shackles. He remained an unsung hero, but he didn't mind. He enjoyed doing his part and that was all the reward he needed. Nevertheless, when he passed, his song was finally sung by a fleet of heartbroken, grateful sailors. A shipmate had fallen, and it was time to honor him for his service.

CAT WAS NUMBER-ONE IN MY LIFE

I am certain that just about everyone in the western hemisphere has heard of Murphy's Law. Murphy's Law states "If anything can go wrong, it will." I, like so many of you, have felt at times that never was there a cliché as accurate as this one. I even agree with the sentiment that was added to this phrase by someone who undoubtedly had much experience with this law. He'd added, "Murphy was an optimist, because not only will something go wrong if it can, but it will go wrong at the worst possible time!"

There are times when I feel that I was adopted and my real surname is actually Murphy. If I was in a two-thousand-square-foot room with nothing in it but myself and a little table in the far corner of the room and I dropped a quarter, it would roll clear across the room and right under that table. And as I reached under to retrieve it, I would most certainly bang my head. That is just the way things happen in my life. I am sure that many of you know what I mean.

Case in point. My wife and I were hurrying to get out of the house. She had to drop the kids off at school and I had to get to work. I was in my dress uniform, and running a little late, so I was in a hurry. Before you think I am an irresponsible employee who cannot manage their time, when I say that I was running late, I meant that I was not as early to leave as I usually was.

In thirty-three years of military service I was never late to work, not once. Often I was there not only early, but very early. I cannot remember now, but since it took me about forty minutes to get from where I lived to the downtown Honolulu federal building where I worked, I was probably leaving ninety minutes before work started. Still, for me, that was cutting it close. So I was rushing, running around helping with getting the kids ready, and trying to get them out the door before I left.

Out the door they went about thirty seconds ahead of me, as I finished washing up the breakfast dishes. I did not hear the front door close and since I could hear the noise from the outside, I knew the kids had left it open again. I yelled after them to close it, but the only response I got was the sound of three car doors closing and the engine of my wife's car starting. Murphy's Law was alive and well.

I finished up the dishes, dried my hands, and walked over to the door to close it. I was greeted by the neighbor's cat, a big yellow tabby. She poked her head in the door and I said, "Good morning."

Apparently, it wasn't such a good morning for her. She jumped when I spoke to her and landed inside the house. Knowing she was a bit spooked, I slowly opened the front door wider and soothingly urged her to exit.

That was not going to happen. She decided it would be more exciting to run around the townhouse in a panicked frenzy. This cat had no feline agility at all. She darted from room to room smashing into furniture and other obstacles as if she was being chased by a pack of large, angry dogs.

She wasn't. Nobody was chasing her. I hadn't moved and wasn't even talking to her any longer. I was in a state of semi-shock at her ridiculous behavior and the unbelievable mess one cat could make in such a short period of time.

Having taken the grand tour of the downstairs of the town-house and somehow still missing the open door, the cat suddenly noticed the drapes. *These,* I am sure she thought, *would provide an excellent way of escape.* In one jump, she sunk her claws into the floor-length drapes and half pulled herself up and half pulled them down.

Eventually, the drapes came crashing down, which only served to fuel her fear more. She then sunk her claws into the stucco wall and climbed upward. I was amazed at how easily she scaled the bare wall. At the top, she wrapped her front legs around the drapery rod holder and just hung there for a moment.

I saw this as an opportunity to gently reach out for her to come down. She saw it as an opportunity to urinate and defecate down the side of the wall. I had no idea a cat could hold so much fluid. Now perhaps you understand the intended twist to the words *number one* in the title of this story. Needless to say, Murphy's Law was in full swing.

Still suspended three quarters of the way up the wall, she spied the stairs leading to the upstairs. Fortunately, at almost exactly the same moment, I noticed that she noticed the stairs and I positioned myself for the jump that I knew was coming. I caught her in midair and her claws dug deep into my arms.

I squeezed her tight to my chest to reduce the amount of damage her claws could do to me and hurried toward the front door.

Once there, I unceremoniously ejected her from the house and turned to see the mess she had made. My entire uniform was soiled with her excrement and I not only had to change, but I also had to shower and clean up the mess she had made. It was certain that I was going to be late. Murphy's Law had come to fruition in my home that day.

As fate would have it, I was not late. Traffic had been light, apparently the only element of my life that had escaped Murphy's Law. I made it to work with a few minutes to spare.

Later that day, tongue in cheek I let the neighbor know that her cat had broken into my house and vandalized it. Her response was classic Murphy's Law. *"Oh my goodness, no wonder she has been so upset today!"*

She's upset? Really?

*AUSTRALIAN DOG GONE MAD

This is not a personal story. In fact, I have no part in the story at all, except to validate that it is true. I have used this story in illustration while teaching one subject or another for many, many years. I wish I could give credit to whoever deserves it, but I have not been able to locate a source. I can only offer that I saw the story more than forty years ago in a publication in Hawaii, and that is about the closest I can pinpoint its origin and authenticity. But it goes like this . . .

A ranch hand in Australia decided to take a dip in the river to cool off during the afternoon heat. After disrobing sufficiently to take a swim, the man started off to a slight bluff overlooking the river where he could dive in to the refreshing water.

As he moved toward the bluff, his dog, which was always by his side, positioned himself in front of him and growled. The man was momentarily taken aback. His dog had never acted this way before. He dismissed the dog by saying, "Move aside mate," and continued on.

The dog again jumped in front of him growling and bearing his teeth in a ferocious manner. The man did not know what to think, but again dismissed the dog, taking a halfhearted swipe at it with his foot. "Get out of the way dawg." Once again, he started for the water.

The dog, apparently out of options, ran in front of the man and jumped in the water ahead of him. The man had no time to wonder about the dog's behavior, because as soon as the dog hit the water, a huge crocodile sprung upon it. The dog cried out in pain as the brute closed its powerful jaws on its back leg.

Calm down. There is a happy ending to this story, unless you are cheering for the crocodile. The man quickly figured out what was happening and reached for his pistol lying nearby on top of his clothes and threw himself right into the mix. He dispatched the crocodile with a single shot to the head. The dog was badly injured, but made a full recovery.

It appears dogs are great everywhere. They may bark with an accent in Australia, but they are just as devoted as ours here in the States.

I TOAD YOU NOT TO EAT THAT

Years ago I brought home my first West Highland White terrier and named her Samantha. Westies are a very tough, sturdy breed. They are also reported to be one of the most intelligent breeds of canines. I am not so sure.

Samantha was a wonderful girl. She is gone now and I miss her every day, but I gave her a good life and have no regrets. I will see her again along with the other pets who have shared my home and life. It will be a grand reunion. Until then, I will do what we all do, plod along the best I can. In some things Sam lived up to the breed's reputation and was quick as a whip, at least in certain protocols. But in other common sense things, she came up a little short. We had an episode with chocolate. One evening, we returned home from church and the kids ran in the house ahead of me. They quickly came running back outside as I finished locking up the car, yelling, "Dad, Sam ate all the chocolate."

The kids had brought home from school those bars of fundraiser chocolate many schools sell once a year. I am sure you are familiar with them. In our absence, Sam had climbed up on the furniture and gotten into one of the boxes. The kids had not exaggerated. She had eaten all of the chocolate, or at least made a very good stab at it.

At least seven bars had remained in the box when we left. When we returned there were no whole bars. Empty wrappers were everywhere—on the sofa, on the table, on the floor, and even stuck to Sam's fur. Only one partially eaten bar was all that remained. Apparently, she had reached her limit at six and a half bars.

She stood in front of me with chocolate all over her white fur, bloated like a parade balloon and wagging her tail as if she had done something good. I was initially worried because it is well known that animals and chocolate are not a good mix, but she weathered the experience without any discomfort other than her gurgling, bloated stomach.

Of course, she was on a sugar high the rest of the night and when Samantha didn't sleep, no one slept. She ran around the house with her nails clicking on the floor and found every possible noise to investigate and bark or growl at. It was especially difficult for me, because when my dogs bark in the middle of the night, it is a signal for me to get up and check things out. I was up a lot that night.

That is just one example of her lack of common sense. There are plenty of others. From drinking from the ocean to attacking dogs five times her size, she just would not be a candidate for doggie Mensa, if there were such a thing.

Perhaps her worst common senseless caper was with the large nonindigenous cane toads found in South Florida, *Bufo marinus*. As everyone knows (except Samantha apparently), when threatened or stressed, these toads squeeze out a very toxic compound around their necks and throats. Though some irresponsible thrill seekers have indulged in the practice of licking such excited toads for a hallucinatory high, the effects of this toxin can most assuredly result in death, especially when it comes to small predatory animals or pets. Many a potential predator has learned this lesson too late.

In the Miami area it is almost impossible for pets to avoid toad contact. At night, you can find a half dozen large toads gathered around a dog food bowl helping themselves to dry dog food. Another dozen will be under the street lamp capitalizing on the insects drawn to the light. The toads are everywhere.

I made a special effort to teach Samantha about these toads. We sat together on several occasions for fifteen or twenty minutes going over the basics. I would agitate the toad or squeeze out the toxin and let Sam smell both. Invariably, she would snap at the toad. That was her nature.

I would emphatically scold her and say, "*No, No,*" over and over again, until I could put the toad down in front of her without her pouncing on it.

The lesson did not stay with her long. Each time I walked this braniac of a breed, she would lunge at any toad that crossed her path. I would sit her down and go through the lesson again. And each time I was sure that she had finally gotten it. After all, she was one of the most intelligent breeds, right?

Well one evening, instead of taking her for a walk like they were supposed to, one of my children tied her to an outside tree and left her there to take care of her business. When I realized what they had done, I quickly rushed outside. It was the time of day when toads began to get active. But I was too late. Sam had already grabbed a toad and tried to kill it. The toad had reacted like toads do and shot out venom to deter the assault.

It worked. Sam was in bad shape. She was frothing at the mouth and staggering, almost unable to stay on her feet. She did not respond to my voice. I knew it was bad, but there was no time to rush her to the veterinarian. I grabbed the hose, turned it

on half power, and shoved it into her mouth. I flushed out whatever venom was still remaining in her mouth and then jammed
my fingers down her throat in an attempt to make her vomit.
She did not vomit, but she did spit out some mucous and yel-
lowish venom.

I left her for a moment to run into the house to get some vine-
gar, which I had been told was a good neutralizer of the toxin.
When I returned, Sam was nowhere to be found. I panicked. Where
had she gone? I had been gone less than a minute.

I knew she could not get far in her condition, but she was so
incoherent she probably had no idea where she was going. I
quickly ran circles around the immediate adjacent houses in the
neighborhood. I looked behind trash cans, under cars, in drainage
ditches. She was nowhere to be found. My heart was sinking in
my chest. I did not know what to do.

I caught a glimpse of something white in the grass where Sam
had been chained up and ran over there. I was relieved to see
that it was her. She had lain down in the deep grass and been
enveloped by it out of my sight. Just the twitch of one of her
ears was all I had caught a glimpse of, but I was thankful I had
seen it.

She looked up at me and wagged her tail, but did not stand.
I knew then that she would make it. Apparently the quick rinse
of her mouth had removed most of the toxin before it was absorbed into her system. In a few moments, she stood and after
a half hour she was her same old self again.

The kids were feeling very badly for having put her in such
danger, but I assured them it was not their fault and that Sam
was going to be fine. Anyway, they had learned an important

lesson in responsibility and I was sure it would never happen again, so why make them feel any worse than they already did.

Sam on the other hand, was a different story. I had hoped this harsh lesson was the element needed in teaching her the danger of cane toads. It was not. On a whim, I located a toad after Sam was feeling better and put it in front of her. She immediately lunged at it and I had to scold her yet again.

I expressed my frustration to my wife later that evening. "One of the most intelligent breeds my eye."

She expertly turned the tables on me. "Well you know honey, those studies are generalized. Other studies show that animals tend to take on the attributes of their humans so I wouldn't be too hard on her."

Ouch!

BUMPER STICKERS
SHOULD BE ILLEGAL

"There's one Grandpa," yelled the oldest of the three grandsons in the car with me. "What does it say, what does it say?"

Without losing my focus on the vehicle in front of us, I glanced quickly over at the bumper of the car in the next lane. It says, "If you can read this bumper sticker you are too close."

To my surprise, instead of the puzzled look I expected from their single-digit age group, the boys all laughed heartily at this clever, time-worn warning. Ordinarily, this type of bland humor goes right over their young heads, so I was impressed by their savvy. It seemed I had some very enlightened grandsons.

My prideful marveling was short-lived however, as another of the three asked, "So why are you so close then, Grandpa?"

"I am not too close," I tried to explain. "I am in a different lane."

"But you are close enough to read it, right?" the youngest of them injected.

"Yes," I responded in frustration that I could not hide. "But the bumper sticker is meant for someone behind them, not for me."

His next response of "Grandpaaaaaaaaaaaa???" reminded me that logic is not always well spent on junior boys. It was apparent he thought I was fibbing to him. I suppose I deserved his doubt for all the times I pretended to pull coins from his ears or snatch thumb-noses from his face. But then, that is what Grandpas do.

It didn't take long for the other two to chime in as they bounced in their safety seats, chanting "Grandpa is too close, Grandpa is too close." How they could rock the entire van while securely fastened by seatbelts remains a mystery to me.

My focus was more on the boys and their taunting than on the traffic ahead of me. Consequently, I had inched too close to the vehicle in front of us. The boys made no mention of that however, as that vehicle had no pseudo-lawful warning on its bumper. Their chorus of condemnation over the bumper sticker on the vehicle in the other lane grew louder and more insistent as they continued to bounce in their safety chairs, chanting, "Grandpa is too close. Grandpa is going to jail."

We had already been to lunch, followed by ice cream, so I could not use those enticements to detour their thinking. My only recourse was to do what any outnumbered grandpa would do . . . I surrendered! I cautiously dropped back a few car lengths until the boys thought I was no longer violating the sacred bumper sticker law.

A sudden chorus of "Yea, Grandpa, you did it" confirmed that I had satisfied their child-like interpretation of the situation and earned their amnesty. All was back to normal and I would not be going to jail. The world was good again. All I had to do was hope there were no other bumper stickers with similar messages (and believe me, they were looking for them) to delay us further. If they were to spot more of that type and I had to again retreat, we might never get home.

I tried to detour their interest from finding more stickers. I suggested the I Spy game, the Quiet game and all the others they had taught me, but none seemed to spark their interest. I made up some lame stories, told a couple silly jokes, and in frustration, even disingenuously offered to let them drive.

They weren't biting. They wanted only to look for more bumper stickers. It had become a cause, their mission. They sang out almost in unison, "Over there Grandpa, that car has one. Go over there and read it." I was driving and reading, explaining and sometimes reexplaining what some of the less clever writings meant.

I was embarrassed by the many lewd and obnoxious presentations, but found comfort in knowing that only one of the boys had begun to read. If the bumper sticker was too risqué, I quickly substituted my own words for what it said and moved away from that vehicle before the one learning to read could sound out the words. When they asked me to explain the one that said *I GOT*

THIS CAR FOR MY WIFE. PRETTY GOOD TRADE HUH? and they didn't understand my explanation, it was time to go home.

I set to that task and blocked out all of their pleas to read other stickers as they spotted them. As an author, I never thought I would find myself saying something like this, but there can be times when it really isn't fun to read.

SOMEHOW MY MOTHER SURVIVED MY CHILDHOOD

I am always amused when I hear my daughter or nieces lament the strange things their junior-aged sons do. From the boys fishing out things they accidentally dropped into the toilet without washing their hands afterwards to vigorously poking a hornet's nest with a short stick, they seem to have an endless list of dumb things to accomplish before succumbing to maturity. It may not be politically correct to say, but boys will be boys.

The truth is that these are not only normal activities for junior boys, but are relatively mild undertakings and nothing to be alarmed about. My mother would have gladly traded places with anyone if that were all she had to deal with, because I kept her life just a little bit more exciting than that.

My mother had three children, but she earned all the stripes of motherhood from me. Before age ten, I had caused her anxiety sufficient for several lifetimes. I am not gloating about that, nor did I purposely try to cause her grief. I simply was a boy. I was in my own world, experiencing life as many young boys do, oblivious to the dangers or ramifications of living life.

To what would later prove to be to my mother's dismay, I discovered nature early in life and loved the creatures that lived there. In particular, as I will discuss in greater detail later in this chapter, I found snakes to be fascinating. The effect they had on my sister and her friends spoke volumes to me about their potential worth. For years, I suffered under the abuse of my older sister. By sheer size, she commanded my conformance to whatever her will dictated. Who could have known that one small snake down her back was all it took for her to give me the respect I yearned for?

Mom was the best. She not only forgave that horrific act, but allowed me to keep my collection of snakes in my room. She had no idea how large my collection had grown until the dozen or so members somehow got loose in the house one evening. Even then, Mom showed amazing restraint, though if you watched closely you could see her hair graying.

I guess it was discovering the box of live scorpions in the storeroom that finally pushed her over the edge. Or maybe it was the fact that I had been stung by them a couple times and said nothing about it. Whatever the catalyst, my whole collection of critters—scorpions, snakes, horny toads, frogs, and turtles—were evicted, at least temporarily. In time, she would acquiesce and allow me to keep them again, minus the scorpions.

She should have known by those early warning signals what was in store for her and put me up for adoption. But somehow, despite my sister's protests, she still wanted to keep me. I laid low for a few weeks, but lacking common sense, it didn't take long for me to find more trouble.

I had purposed to go straight, but in less than thirty days I was arrested for climbing a restricted fence on a naval base where I was exposed to radiation. I climbed over to pet the guard dog. He let me come over, wagging his tail and licking my face. I would say he was more to blame than I was for not doing his job. The base police did not see it that way.

Scolded thoroughly by them and my father, I once again determined that my days of trouble were over. That lasted another week, when my friend and I unearthed a metal chest down near where ships tie up. We were innocently exploring a trash heap as boys do and found what we were sure was a treasure chest full of emeralds and other precious gems.

The fact that the chest was full of emergency day and night flares and flare pistols was not anticlimactic for us. We eagerly and excitedly loaded the pistols and began shooting flares all over the bay. For some reason, the Naval Police didn't like us doing that, either! They were very hard to please. I never knew they arrested little kids so much! Don't they have better things to do?

Though there are easily a hundred stories of this type that I could share, space requires that I just jump ahead and tell you about "The Day." That is the name it came to be known by around our house. Without doubt, my mother could trump all the collective worries and misgivings of my daughter and four nieces by sharing with them her trauma and frustrations on "The Day."

In our family, that day is akin to Pearl Harbor in that it lives in infamy. It was the day I pulled the biggest bonehead stunt of my young life. Of course, I didn't think it was at the time. Indeed, it was just another adventure.

We lived in Vallejo, California, and I was in the fifth grade.

One afternoon, my friend suggested we go to the hills across the valley in Napa the next day instead of going to school. Somehow, in my young mind, that sounded like a great idea. We had always wanted to see those hills. Since we planned to be gone about the same amount of time we would have been in school, we figured no one would be the wiser.

There was no malice aforethought and no intent to upset or hurt anyone. There was no thought of ramifications or fallout. We were just employing the cognitive powers junior boys are equipped with and hatching what was undoubtedly a stellar plan.

Anxious to go, my friend, I, and his younger brother rose before sunrise and headed out. I didn't think my mother would miss me at breakfast, because she seldom got up that early. So we were good to go, and go we did.

The five mile trip across the valley took considerably longer than our experienced fifth grade minds had calculated. We had to cross about a dozen waterways, commonly called sloughs, and that was no easy task. It required scaling fences, wading, swimming, and climbing under water pump houses. Nothing we could not handle, just unexpected delays.

We eventually arrived in Napa. It was well into the afternoon by the time we got there. Wet and cold from our repeated crossing of the sloughs, we enjoyed the warm sun as we climbed the coveted hills, which, by the way, had grown considerably larger in size upon our approach. No matter, there was adventure to be had, so we forged ahead.

We thoroughly enjoyed our day, even the brief bout with quicksand and my being bitten by a large, unidentified snake in retaliation for grabbing it by the tail. None of that was of any concern to us. We were on top of the world. Nothing was going to ruin our day.

Unfortunately, there was one factor we had not considered—time. The sun was quickly dropping in the sky and even though we knew we hadn't a prayer of getting home around the time school let out, we quickly scurried back toward the sloughs.

Long after dark we finally came up out of the last canal. We would have hurried home, but our attention was diverted to a commotion at the local lake about a quarter mile from where we were.

Police cars, ambulances, fire trucks, news crews, and several hundred people were gathered at one end of the lake. Men in boats in the water and search lights from the big trucks illuminated the water where they were searching. All the flashing lights and crowds of people made it look almost like a carnival.

We hurried over to the lake to find out what was going on. We had already forgotten that we were probably in trouble for being late. There was a carnival going on. But as we worked our way through the crowd, it dawned on us that this was no carnival.

I saw a friend of mine straddling his bike and I called out to him. "Hey Billy. Hey Billy. What's going on?"

Billy turned toward me and his face immediately went pale. Despite his obvious shock, he came closer and managed to say excitedly, "Gary, what are you doing here? You are in such trouble. Your mom and dad and the whole neighborhood have been looking for you all day. The school called to say you had not shown up today. They didn't know if you had been kidnapped or what. They are dragging the lake for your body. You have had it, my friend!"

I was now pale. I turned to run home, but Billy stopped me. He told me that he needed to take me because there was a reward for information about me and he wanted it. I was tired anyway, so I agreed to his giving me a ride. We arrived at my house and all I remember amidst all the commotion my arrival caused is the shriek that my mother let out. I have never been hugged so hard in all my life as she hugged me that day. For a moment, I felt like the most loved kid in the world.

Unfortunately, that feeling was short-lived. Whatever relief my mother felt from seeing me quickly dissipated and was replaced by anger, perhaps even rage. Suddenly, I felt like the most hated kid in the world as my mother scolded me using language that I never heard her use before, language that would embarrass a sailor.

I know that to be true, because my dad was a sailor at the time, a Chief in the Navy, and he was wincing at the words coming out of her mouth, but still anxiously waiting for his turn with me. Well, no need to finish that story. I am sure you can fill in the blanks. Suffice it to say that I did very little sitting down for a while.

So mothers, if your sons are driving you crazy, or if they seem to lack the common sense that you feel they should possess, don't be overly concerned. They aren't weird or maladjusted. They are just boys, and at that age boys will be boys. There is no getting around it. The next time your son does something that you think is gross or idiotic, measure it by the behavior my mother had to endure. It might not seem so bad after all.

For the record, "The Day" was a topic I did not bring up for many, many years. Others in the family were free to mention it and make fun of my stupidity, but I was not allowed to chuckle along with them unless I wanted to relive all over again the hurt that I caused.

Many years later, as my mother and father were visiting our church on a day that I was speaking, I took the opportunity to publically recount "The Day" and to offer an adult apology for the child foolishness I visited upon them.

They were very moved and so forgiving that even I could make jokes about "The Day" from then on.

BLACK AND BLUE HAWAII

"My goodness honey, what on Earth are those?" my wife asked as she pointed to my legs. By the seriousness of her expression, I looked down expecting to see a horde of creepy critters crawling up my legs. As it turned out, a series of large bruises covered the inside of both my legs.

We probably would not have noticed them if it weren't for the fact that we were in our swimming attire. We had just come out of the water at Kuhio Beach, Waikiki and my legs were exposed. When we are back home in Hawaii, we usually get up at sunrise each morning and go to the beach to swim.

It is a great time to swim because it is cool out, at least by is-

land standards, and we are virtually alone on the beach. The locals do not have tolerance for the morning cold and the tourists
don't usually get up that early. The coolness didn't bother us because we were used to a more northern climate in Kansas, where
we lived at the time.

As I examined the bruises more closely, I became a bit concerned. It wasn't just one or two bruises, but rather twelve of
them. That made me a bit worried. A friend of mine had unexpectedly contracted leukemia while deployed overseas as a Mer-
chant Marine. The first indication of his having the disease was
a series of bruises covering his body. Since I had spent so much
time with him in the hospital during his recovery, I was pretty
sensitive to unexplained bruises.

Upon closer examination, I discovered that the six bruises on
my right inside leg matched almost exactly the six bruises on my
left inside leg. This suggested to me that the bruises were caused
by something external and not an internal problem. I breathed
a sigh of relief upon that realization, but kept it to myself until
I could figure out where the bruises came from. I knew that my
wife would not feel relieved until I could explain how they happened.

My wife asked if I had hurt myself in some way. I answered
in the negative. I was sure that I had not. Admittedly, I can hurt
myself and not really be aware of it. I just don't feel the pain
right away. For instance, I can run my thigh hard into a desk and
just bounce off it without any pain. The soreness and bruise
comes later. But I was sure that nothing like that had happened.

I reexamined the bruises and discovered that they were all circular in shape and of varying sizes. Each matched the bruises of varying sizes on the opposite leg. This was most curious.

As I thought about the shapes and position of the bruises, I suddenly remembered how and where I had gotten them. Three days earlier, we had landed at Honolulu International Airport. At this point, I need to mention that I am not comfortable flying. In particular, I am most uncomfortable during landings. Watching the airport buildings and other structures zip by always makes me feel as if we will never be able to stop.

Involuntarily, and almost without my consciously realizing it, during the landing I had wrapped my legs around the seat and squeezed, my only outward reaction to the inward terror I was feeling. I pressed my legs against the sides of the chair, bearing down with all my strength for at least a minute, until I felt the after thruster kick in and the plane begin to slow significantly. The bruises coincide exactly with the contact points my legs made with the chair.

You don't think I told my wife that right away, do you? Oh no. I have been married much too long to let a golden opportunity like that go by. I said in a soft, and if I might add, pathetic voice, "I don't know what is wrong. All I can think of is how Harold (my friend) had these same bruises when he was diagnosed with leukemia."

My wife is a wonderful woman and she treats me well, but that day the attention she showed me was extra special for some reason. Okay, I determined that I would suddenly remember where I got the bruises later that day and let her off the hook, but for the time being I wanted to milk the situation for all the sympathy I could get. What did you expect? I am a man after all.

*GERI'S KIDS

As a career Coast Guard officer, I am big on boating safety. Boating accidents can be as grisly and fatal as automobile accidents and those who sail or motor should be as prepared and experienced to drive their boat as they are their automobile.

A good illustration of how important boating safety and preparation is comes from a source close to home for me, a coworker and friend named Geri. Her husband had taken their two grandchildren, ages two and five, out in his motorboat at a protected lagoon on Oahu. As grandma (Geri) stood on the shore, grandpa and grandkids would occasionally go zooming by. Each time they did my friend would wave and throw kisses to them.

After a few passes, grandpa turned the boat into the channel that led to the open sea. Several large swells were coming into the lagoon, most likely from a passing vessel, and he apparently wanted to give the grandkids a thrill riding up and down the rolling swells. As the boat powered over one of the swells, it took a hard jolt from a second wave and to grandma's horror the impact caught her husband off guard and knocked him out of the boat.

She was mortified. The boat headed rapidly toward the mouth of the lagoon and the open ocean. Her husband was in the water far behind the boat and her two young grandchildren were alone onboard. If the boat veered to either side of the channel, it would crash into the rock jetties or telephone pole day markers sticking out of the water.

At the speed the boat was going, it undoubtedly would disintegrate upon impact and quite possibly explode. If somehow it managed to navigate safely out the channel, it would be immediately exposed to the open ocean. The breaking waves outside the lagoon would quickly capsize and smash the vessel.

She was overcome with this terror unfolding before her eyes and screamed loudly and repeatedly, but there was no one to hear her or to offer the quick help that was needed. She did not know what to do. All she could do was watch in horror as her grandchildren headed toward almost certain death.

Suddenly, miraculously, the boat slowed. It then turned completely around and sped up again. Soon it was alongside her husband and it slowed again. She watched as her husband climbed onboard, took the helm, and headed the boat back to shore. This scene of redemption was almost as shocking as the previous one of terror. She was so numbed by the trauma she had just experienced that she could hardly move to meet the boat as it slid to rest on the sandy beach.

She eventually moved and met the boat as it slid to a stop. She scooped up her grandchildren and smothered them with hugs and kisses. Then she looked searchingly at her husband for some kind of explanation as to what she had just witnessed.

Sensing for the first time her emotional stress, her husband simply said, "Oh, I taught the boy how to drive the boat months ago." When grandpa fell overboard, the young lad simply took the controls and did what grandpa had taught him to do

This is a true story with a very happy ending thanks to the sea-worthy responsibility of one individual. This story is repeated too many times with less than happy results. Take time to ensure every person onboard knows how to operate the vessel, even the youngsters. It might just save a life.

THE HOT ROOM

Like everyone, I have hobbies that occupy my free time (softball, hiking, studying the Bible, writing). Without question, one of my pet hobbies is herpetology, the study of reptiles. I love reptiles, in particular snakes. I understand that socially speaking, even though there seems to be a lot more interest in reptiles today than when I was a boy, it is still not a hobby embraced or even understood by most.

I am often asked why I got interested in snakes. I suppose it was a combination of things. First, I usually lived in an area where it was easy for me to get outside, into the wild, and hike. I was in their backyard, so to speak. They intrigued me. Initially, my interest was in frogs and turtles, but eventually my passion was snakes.

The next reason I can offer is that I was always enamored with their beauty. Seventy percent of the more than 2,700 snakes in the world are extremely colorful. Some have colors that are breathtaking. Others are effervescent with almost 3-D hues, such as the appropriately named Brazilian Rainbow Boa.

Many authors in this field of study appropriately describe these creatures as "Nature's jewelry." My favorite is the family Lampropeltis, or King snakes. The scientific name means "shiny skin," and indeed they are.

Finally, as I alluded to earlier, snakes give a young boy power. Prior to my interest in snakes, I was regularly bullied and roughed up by my older sister and her girlfriends. Admittedly, I was a pest and probably deserved everything they did to me, but that is the hindsight of a mature adult speaking.

As a ten-year-old, anything and everything they did to me was undeserved and grounds for revenge. And oh my, the revenge was sweet. From the moment I pulled the three foot California King snake out of the box and put it down my fifteen-year-old sister's back, I commanded respect. I was never pushed, slapped, bitten, or screamed at again. Is there anyone who cannot see the worth to these wonderful creatures?

Move the clock forward about twenty years. I was living in Florida on the edge of the Everglades, one of the most exciting places on Earth for someone who loves to be out in nature. I hadn't kept reptiles for many years because I had lived in the northern United States. But conditions were conducive in Florida to keeping an active collection for the purpose of maintaining a breeding and release program.

I was cofounder of the Miami Everglades Herpetological Society and was involved in several ongoing public education programs, which made it nearly impossible not to keep certain animals. I no longer house reptiles because of the commitment of time and expense that proper husbandry requires, but then I maintained a very large collection.

It amused me when friends or coworkers would stop by the house and realize that I had a collection of indigenous and exotic snakes.

Their first reaction was invariably, "Eww, snakes? How disgusting!" Without exception, the next thing out of their mouth was, "Can I see them?" That was almost always followed by, "Can I touch one?"

And so, I could mark another notch in my "educate the public" belt. I cannot honestly recall how many friends told me that because of the education I gave them, they would no longer kill a snake, but rather let it go on its way unmolested. They understood their worth in the ecosystem and the silliness of the many fables about them.

And I said all that to get to my story about the Hot Room. On weekends, a friend in the reptile import business entrusted me with the running of his shop. I did this for approximately eight years and always enjoyed caring for the hundreds of creatures we housed and raised.

On one particular morning in 1988, I opened the shop early to get some cleaning work done. Something felt wrong, but nothing seemed to be out of place. Sometimes when a large lizard like a Nile Monitor escaped during the night, it would make a mess of things, turning over cages and just generally causing chaos in the shop. But nothing like was that visible so I dismissed the feeling.

A few minutes later, I noted the light in the Hot Room was not on. That is where my friend kept the venomous or hot animals. It was odd that I could not see the light shining out from under the locked door. The timer always turned the lights on before we arrived in the mornings.

I was not supposed to go into the room without my friend being present, but it seemed like an emergency to me. I used a knife to wedge the locked door open and reached for the timer.

As I did, I heard a nasty *"hissssss"* from the center of the room. Ordinarily, reaching for the timer is a simple task and it takes a mere second to find it and spin it until the lights come on. But after that hiss, I was not concentrating on the apparatus, but rather staring into the dark apprehensively so it took a few seconds longer.

When I spun the dial, the lights flashed on and I saw a cobra in hooded position in the middle of the room about eight feet from where I was standing, which was a pretty safe distance. Unfortunately, I had spun the dial too far. The lights had come on and then immediately went off again. But it was long enough for me to see at least one agitated animal on the loose.

Well, I quickly spun the dial again, and the lights came on and stayed on. I was aghast at what I saw. Hot cages were overturned all around the room, locks still intact, but the glass smashed. As I looked at the mess, keeping an eye on the cobra, I noted other critters moving around under the shelves, including a large Gaboon viper and a moderately sized eastern diamondback rattler. Without turning my head, I reached behind me, grabbed a hook, and started to make my way around the room.

I would have handled the problem myself, but fortunately my friend came in and together we rounded up all the escapees without incident. We pieced together the clues and discovered that a large python had somehow gotten out of her cage in another room, gone up into the overhead and broken down through the ceiling of the Hot Room. Climbing around like the clumsy oafs pythons can often be, she pushed cages out of her way as she moved around the room. They fell off the shelves and broke open. But it was a problem we easily handled.

I was sufficiently reprimanded by my friend for entering the room without him having been present. Not the way I like to start my day, but at least on this day I didn't need coffee to get me started.

YOU WON'T BELIEVE THIS ONE

In the summer of 1985 in Miami, Florida, my wife and I were sitting alone at the breakfast table.

"What's wrong honey," my wife asked from across the breakfast table. "You don't look well. Are you okay?"

I nodded to her in almost mechanical response, but I was far from okay. I slowly lowered the Sunday *Parade* magazine, pointing at an artist's conception of an unknown creature recently spotted in the northern New Jersey woods. "You aren't going to believe this, but . . .", and then I told her my story.

Twenty-seven years earlier in 1958 my family lived in rural northern New Jersey. One day my older sister and several of her friends were taking a hike deep into the woods near our home. As an eight year old, I was not welcome among her group of borderline teens. Indeed, my sister gave me strict orders not to bother them. So like any troublesome and irreverent little brother, I followed from a distance and endured the occasional and expected scolding. "Go home, you little brat!"

Some distance into the forest, I got detached from the main group. Whether I took a wrong turn or they were purposely hiding from me I don't know, but I suddenly realized that I could no longer see the group, and I panicked. I ran to where I thought they had been, but they were not there. I thought I heard a noise coming from the other side of a small hill, so I quickly ran around it hoping I would see my sister and her friends.

As I came around the hill, I stopped dead in my tracks. Twenty feet in front of me was someone or something I had never seen before. I can only describe it as a creature shaped like a man, but it was not a man. It was slender and tall, but I cannot say how tall. Everyone is tall to an eight year old. I just know it was a lot taller than my dad and he was a pretty big man.

It wore no clothes, but was covered in dark hair and leaves, emphasis on the leaves. Of all its features it is the head I remember most clearly. Its face was human-like, but it was framed with a border of leaves, much like the hair of a lion's mane. I remember that the leaves did not seem to be ornamental like a garland, but appeared to be part of the creature's anatomy. I cannot describe it better than that. That is what my perception was in the short amount of time I spent looking at the creature.

Undoubtedly, those of you who believe my story are thinking "Bigfoot," but this was 1958. No one had ever heard that term before. And to be honest, I do not remember taking time to look at his feet anyway.

The stories of how people freeze when they are afraid or try to scream but cannot most definitely did not apply to me that day. I let out a piercing scream while turning and running without even the slightest hesitation. I did not look back. I just kept picking them up and putting them down with no thought of ever stopping.

I don't know how much time passed, but it seemed like only seconds before my sister and her friends were at my side. In tears,

I told them what had happened. Of course, they laughed at me in disbelief, but it was a nervous laughter. They could see the terror in my eyes and knew I had seen something out of the ordinary.

Without a word, the whole group seemed to sense that it was time to leave the woods and we collectively started walking in the direction from which we had come. Soon the walk picked up pace as no one apparently wanted to be the one at the end of the line. Ultimately the walk turned into a gallop and by the time we could see the first house, it was an all out race to get out of the woods.

Over the years I eventually buried that encounter deep in my memory. On the rare occasion that it resurfaced I would dismiss the episode as the product of a child's imagination. But that morning at the breakfast table, when I opened that magazine, imagine my shock to see the very face I had seen so many years earlier staring right back at me.

The picture was an artist's conception from eyewitnesses who had seen this creature in the northern New Jersey woods over a period of many years. It matched perfectly in every detail my memory of the creature I had seen and brought memories of that eerie experience flooding back to me.

The impact of seeing that picture was overwhelming. Even though I was an adult and living in Miami 1,500 miles away, it made the hair on my neck stand up. I suppose it was my quiet gasp and sudden pale color that made my wife notice something was amiss. She listened to my story with great interest and empathy, but it was clear that she had her doubts about my recollection of the facts.

"After all," she said, "you were only eight years old. Maybe you heard a story about this creature at a Cub Scout campfire?" I couldn't disagree with her. I was only a child at the time and children often blend reality and imagination. In fact, for that very reason I had doubted my own memories of what I had seen . . . until I opened that newspaper and the campfire story was staring back at me.

See Ya Later, Alligator

My first experience at tagging alligators in Everglades National Park was predictably a memorable one. As memorable as the excitement of dragging alligators out of the water, were the idiosyncrasies of the professor in charge of the program. Though I considered him a friend, he was definitely an oddball. He will remain nameless to avoid embarrassment, for him and for me.

With him, everything had to be done by the numbers. We had to rise at a certain time (tagging is usually done after midnight because gators are more active then). We had to sit in assigned seats in the van. And when the van was parked, everything in the mobile lab was set up in a certain way and there could be no deviations. Critters were weighed, clipped to reflect our research number, and data collected.

I was assigned a certain task and that was all I did. I could not help anyone else for any reason and I could never be in a place other than where I was supposed to be. It was rather sterile and boring.

Later on, I became an alligator handler in my own right and

was competent enough to dive on a gator all by myself. I seldom did, unless I was teaching my son or one of his friends how to handle an alligator safely.

But this first night I was to pretend that I was somewhat of a novice and was to adhere to the whims of the professor. We were not allowed to question established facts, policy, or procedure, either.

For instance, our mission was to capture and weigh as many young alligators as we could, recording any existing research markings, or adding our own for future studies. After observing the routine, I asked the professor what we would do if the mother of one of these gatorlings decided to respond to the distress calls all the young ones were making.

My question was met with dead silence. Everyone stopped what they were doing. Had the new guy actually violated the cardinal rule of asking the professor a procedure contingency question? I was expecting the silence to be followed by a sound verbal chastisement, but instead the professor spoke up. "That will never happen. We are professionals and have taken precautions to have the van outside the interest zone of potential mothers. Besides, there is no way an alligator could get up into the van."

I was not actually a novice around alligators. I had removed several from ponds near the house and relocated them. I had also rescued several from becoming road kill on Tamiami Trail, one of the main arteries through the Everglades. I don't know how to put this diplomatically, so I will just say straight out that the professor's position on mother alligators was pooh pooh. I did not agree with him at all.

And sure enough, perhaps an hour later the four person team

was busy weighing and marking a juvenile alligator when right outside the van we were startled by a strong *"Hissssss."* It was Mama. There was no mistaking it.

The professor said, "Hmmm. It seems I may have miscalculated . . . ."

Before he could finish his sentence mayhem broke out. Mama began climbing into the van and the good professor exited out the driver's door. The rest of us handled the situation. We got control of Mama and moved her back to the water, releasing junior with her.

I remained friends with the professor and helped him on some endangered species projects after that, but I never accepted another invitation to go gator tagging again. I like alligators, but not enough to jump in the water with them at two a.m. Besides, even though I was career military, I am not that regimented an individual to conform to all those silly rules.